Kilobyte couture

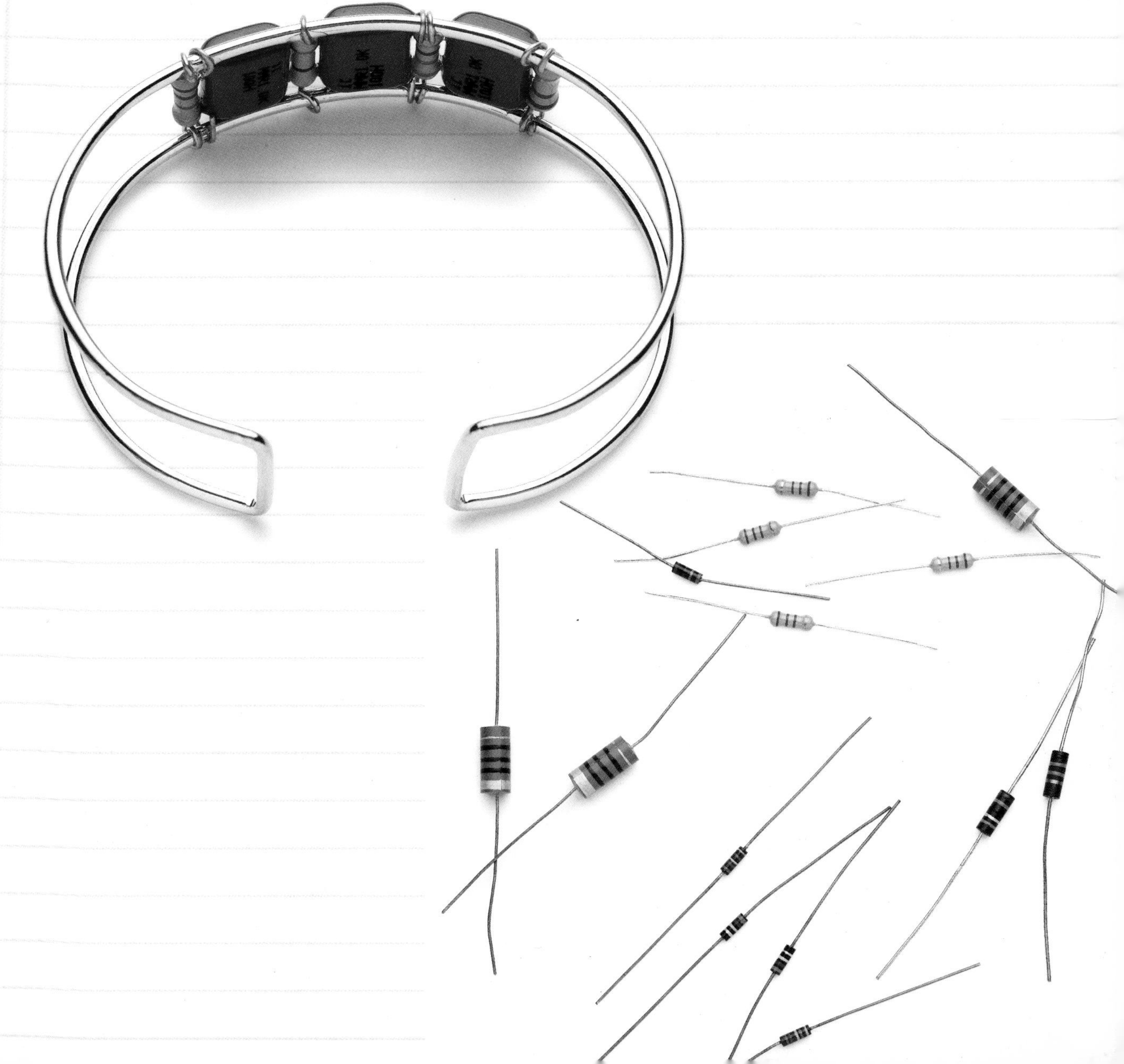

Kilobyte couture

GEEK CHIC JEWELRY TO MAKE FROM EASY-TO-FIND COMPUTER COMPONENTS

Watson-Guptill Publications / New York

BRITTANY FORKS

First published in 2009 by Watson-Guptill Publications, an imprint of the Crown Publishing Group, a division of Random House Inc., New York
www.crownpublishing.com
www.watsonguptill.com

Library of Congress Cataloging-in-Publication Data

Forks, Brittany.
Kilobyte couture : geek chic jewelry to make from easy-to-find computer components / Brittany Forks.
p. cm.
Includes index.
ISBN 978-0-8230-9902-3 (pbk. : alk. paper)
1. Jewelry making. 2. Recycling (Waste, etc.) 3. Art and computers. I. Title.
TT213.F67 2009
745.594'2—dc22
2008040428

SENIOR EDITOR > JULIE MAZUR

PROJECT EDITOR > AMY VINCHESI

ART DIRECTOR > JESS MORPHEW

DESIGNER > MARGO MOONEY

PRODUCTION DIRECTOR > ALYN EVANS

Printed in China

First printing, 2009

1 2 3 4 5 6 7 8 9 / 15 14 13 12 11 10 09 08 07

Acknowledgments

The chance to go through the book-writing process was a new and exciting adventure for me, and I am so glad that I had so many people to guide me. Without these people, I never would have made it through! It has truly been a joy to work with the Watson-Guptill team: Thanks to my wonderful acquisitions editor, Julie Mazur, for finding me and having faith in me that I could create something so beautiful; Amy Vinchesi molded my words into something so much more elegant and witty—without her this book wouldn't be so well written; Margo Mooney did a wonderful job designing the look of the book and laying out all the pages; and Tamara Staples took the most beautiful photos for the interior and was just a total joy to work with.

My family and friends are so completely wonderful and offered advice and endless inspiration throughout the process. My parents and my sister were a constant comfort, helping and offering their opinions without fail. Thank you to Kate and Clifton for guiding me, and for just being the best teachers ever. My best friend, Josh Doty, always edited for me and made sure I made sense. David Warren, the official Senior Citizen of Kilobyte Couture, helped me get the website off the ground and hosted Kilobyte Couture for a while, and is a constant inspiration in all things nerdy. So many more people shaped the ideas around this book and gave me invaluable input and advice, and none of them should go without notice: Jamen Berk, Allie Forks, Steph Rahl, Will Bryant, Mary Beth McDavid, Shannon Rhodes, Gracie Nichols, Luke Abel, Nick Moore, Shanaé Becker, the Plotters, and the entire art department at Mississippi State University.

This book is dedicated to my family and friends: Without you, I wouldn't be here.

Contents

BOOTING UP

geek \ gēk \ *n* 1. an intelligent but single-minded expert in a particular technical field or profession. Usually used self-referentially as a term of pride.

If you think the word "**geek**" only refers to a band hall full of awkward teenagers sporting taped-up glasses, braces, and pigtails—think again! Everybody is a geek in his or her own way.

I became a geek long before I knew what a geek was. I first knew I was different from other kids when I realized I preferred drawing and creating things over going to PE. I was the only kid in my whole class who hated PE, so I wondered what was wrong with me. Why didn't I want to play freeze tag? It was also around this time that our family bought our first computer (it was a Tandy). It had a color screen, unlike our outdated Apple IIs at school; and I spent many hours of my free time using the Paint program and acquainting myself with all the computer's ins and outs. I was always scheming up something; and in the time not spent in front of the computer, I was building a robot suit out of cardboard boxes, constructing a super-elaborate house out of LEGOs, or devising a way to get my parents to buy me Super Nintendo for Christmas. The geek tendency to love the newest and neatest gadgets was rooted early and deeply. I spent a lot of my childhood reading *Nintendo Power*, the Little House series, Dr. Seuss, and myriad other great, geeky things. This fueled my drawing inspiration; I loved nothing more than to have a pencil and paper in front of me. I drew my friends and family, schematics for future projects, and imaginary mystical objects. Luckily, I had a grandmother who shared a love of all things crafty and who fully encouraged any artistic or creative tangent I had chosen to follow each day.

It wasn't until I became a teenager that my identity went through a little crisis, as I developed a love of fashion. I still loved computers and learning HTML, and I actually built my first computer in the eleventh grade. But I also lived for my monthly subscription of *Seventeen* magazine. I was smitten by all the great clothes and cute accessories and how they mixed and matched all the pieces just so to create that perfect outfit. The Back-to-School issue was my favorite: I always tried to bookmark all the best outfits for that crucial Back-to-School shopping expedition. So it seemed a conflict was born: Was I a true geek or a trendsetting fashionista?

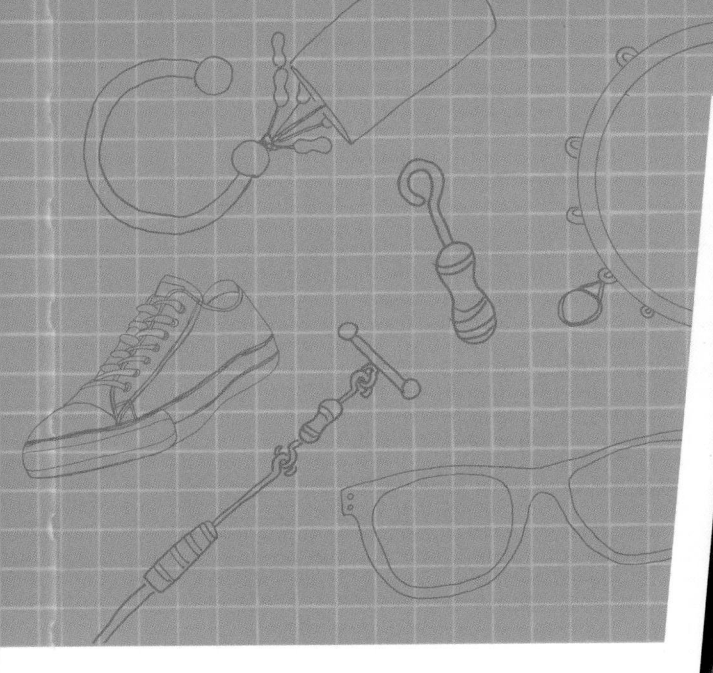

Everybody is a geek in his or her own way, and being geek chic is all about staying true to yourself while looking totally cute and fashionable.

geek chic \ gēk shēk \ *n* 1. fashion designed for or by computer enthusiasts.

When I got to college, I discovered the solution to my great conflict on the Internet: the **geek chic** movement. It embodied me perfectly. You may be wondering, "What is geek chic?" I'm *thrilled* you asked! Geek chic is a movement that focuses on taking uncool or "nerdy" things and making them 100 percent cute. The trend is all about staying true to your geeky tendencies while looking glamorous and fashionable. Geek chic is hot and gaining devotees all the time, as more girls and young women than ever before are learning computer languages, becoming engineers, loving the sciences, and playing video games. Geeky girls are smart, spirited, creative, motivated, and even a dash irreverent; most of all, we're not shy about pursuing our own interests and personal style—be it quirky, cool, or downright eccentric. And even if you don't consider yourself geeky, you can still be geek chic! It's a supercute look, no matter who wears it. Geek chic can be as simple as Converse Chuck Taylors and a great pair of glasses, or as varied as Tina Fey's wardrobe—which spans everything from jeans and T-shirts to red-carpet cocktail dresses. I consider Tina one of the chicest of geeks: She is true to herself (one of the most important aspects of any look) and her upbringing, while looking gorgeous every time I see her. Other geek chic staples include argyle prints, sweater vests, cardigans, and vintage jewelry. I understand how some of these pieces may seem a little boring on their own; but if there's one thing I learned from *Seventeen*, it's that it's all in how you wear them. You can't go wrong with a fitted, brightly colored sweater vest, a unique tie, jeans, and Converse!

For most of my college career I worked in the Electrical and Computer Engineering building. This gave me access to more geeks and computers than I could shake a stick at. I loved the fact that if I had a computer problem, I could just ask

more

All signs point to cool—here Shanaé models the Gigaburst Ring (see page 88).

around until I found somebody who was an expert. One day at work I found a box of old resistors and capacitors, and they came in such beautiful colors: sky blue, bright orange, and sea foam green. I immediately wanted to make something with these spare parts, but what? Then it hit me: jewelry! I quickly went to the craft store and bought a few tools, and then came back and started crafting. At first I just gave my pieces to friends and family; but after a while the idea came to me to put them on the Internet, so I began selling my little creations on Etsy.com. To my delight they sold well, and so I took it to the next level by building a professional website. Thus, Kilobyte Couture was born.

Whether you love geekery or fashion—or both—this book is for you. The twenty-five earrings, necklaces, rings, and other adornments are all made with new and unused electronic components—you know, the things found in computers, TVs, radios, and almost every electronic device imaginable. They're all easy to complete and can be made in only one or two hours. There are projects for nearly everyone on your list, from your littlest cousin to your best friend to your grandmother—not to mention yourself!

Even if you're already well programmed in the jewelry-making arts, I recommend at least skimming the introductory chapter to familiarize yourself with the basic materials and techniques used in this book. The projects themselves are split up according to jewelry type. Each chapter increases in difficulty as you go, but none are very hard, so you can begin crafting anywhere you wish. And don't feel as if you have to stick to these projects exactly! Feel free to check out the "Customizing Your App" suggestions in each project for ideas to make the piece more unique. The materials listed are just guidelines. If you want to use a chunkier resistor than what is called for, go for it! It's all about making the piece your own.

Once you master the basic techniques, you can use these parts to make almost anything—belts, cuff links, even tiaras. Look through fashion magazines and study electronic parts catalogs. Come up with your own wild and crazy applications for geek chic jewelry. If you like a technique I used on a pair of earrings but would prefer a pendant, make it happen! This is the perfect springboard to flex your creative nerd chops. When you come up with something you love, upload a picture to the gallery at www.kilobytecouture.com and show off your geeky skills!

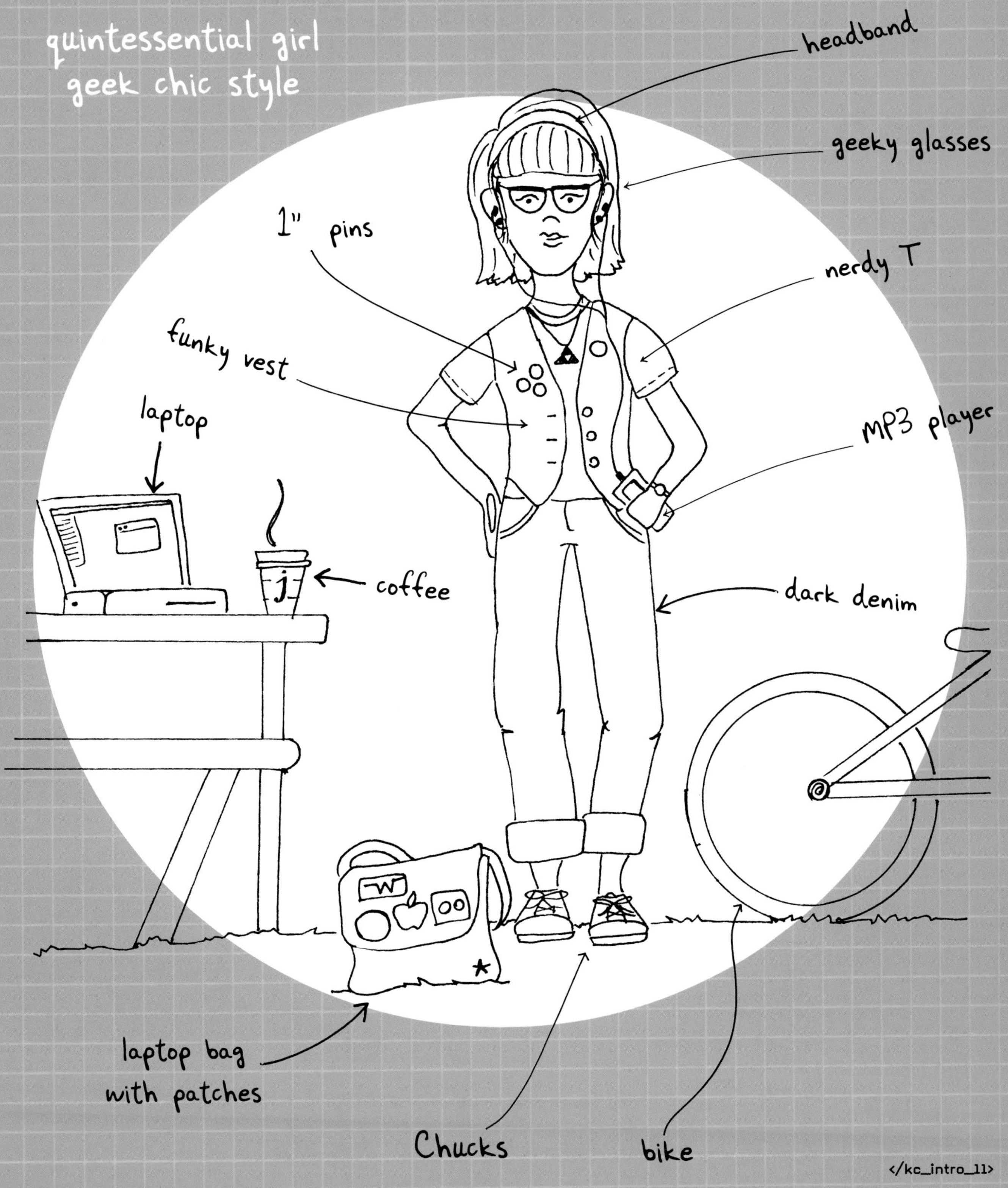
quintessential girl
geek chic style
headband
geeky glasses
1" pins
nerdy T
funky vest
laptop
MP3 player
coffee
j
dark denim
W
laptop bag
with patches
Chucks
bike

</kc_intro_11>

GEEK TIME LINE

1895 > The first radio signal is transmitted

1896 > IBM is established

1901 > The keypunch machine is developed, which is the precursor to computers as we know them

1907 > The first radio broadcasts are established

1917 > Converse launches the Chuck Taylor All-Stars shoe

1927 > Television is first demonstrated in the United States

1935 > IBM introduces the electric typewriter

1938 > Hewlett-Packard (HP) is formed by William Hewlett and David Packard

1939 > The first computer using binary arithmetic is developed by John Vincent Atanasoff

1945 > The first computer "bug" is discovered

1946 > The University of Pennsylvania unveils the ENIAC (Electronic Numerical Integrator and Computer), the first general-purpose electronic computer

1949 > John Mauchly creates Short Order Code, thought to be the first high-level programming language

1952 > Grace Murray Hopper creates the first compiler, known as "A-0"

1955 > The concept of Artificial Intelligence is created

1957 > Sputnik 1 is launched by the Soviet Union

1958 > Willy Higinbotham develops the first video game, *Tennis for Two*

1959 > Xerox introduces the commercial copy machine

1961 > A student at MIT creates *Spacewar*, the first interactive video game

1962 > Perdue and Stanford Universities establish Computer Science Departments

1964 > The computer language known as Basic is developed and put into use

1964 > Dr. Douglas C. Engelbart invents the computer mouse

1965 > Frank Herbert's *Dune* is published

1965 > Moore's Law is coined, which states that technological advancements will double approximately every two years

1966 > *Star Trek* begins airing on TV

1967 > Texas Instruments introduces its first handheld calculator

1969 > The first four nodes of ARPANET (the precursor of the Internet) become operational

1970 > *The Computer Group News*, the first computer enthusiast magazine, is established

1970 > The floppy disk makes its debut

1971 > Intel 4004, the first microprocessor, debuts, which changes personal computing forever

1971 > The first e-mail message is sent

1972 > Nolan Bushnell (later the creator of *Pong*) founds Atari

1972 > The first word-processing programs are introduced

1974 > The first edition of *Dungeons and Dragons* (D&D) is released

1974 > Plans for the first personal computer are published in *Radio Electronics*

1977 > Atari releases the Atari 2600 home gaming system

1977 > Apple Computer is incorporated

1977 > *Star Wars* is released

1977 > Bill Gates founds Microsoft

1978 > *Battlestar Galactica* premiers on TV

1978 > Midway releases *Space Invaders* into arcades

1979 > The first *Hitchhiker's Guide to the Galaxy* book is published

1979 > Cellular phones begin testing in limited markets

1980 > Pac-Man fever sweeps the country, with 300,000 units sold

1981 > *Electronic Games* debuts, the first magazine dedicated to video games

1982 > *Time* magazine names the computer as "Man of the Year"

1982 > The first commercial e-mail service is established in major U.S. cities

1983 > The Internet becomes globally linked

1984 > MacPaint is unveiled for the Macintosh

1984 > The CD-ROM is developed by Sony and Phillips

1984 > The term "cyberspace" is coined by William Gibson

1985 > *Tetris* is developed for the PC

1985 > Windows 1.0 debuts

1985 > *Ender's Game*, by Orson Scott Card, is published

1985 > PageMaker, the first desktop publishing program, debuts on the Macintosh

1986 > The Nintendo Entertainment System (NES) comes to the U.S.

1986 > Sega releases the Sega Master System to compete with the NES

1988 > Internet Relay Chat (IRC) is created in Finland by Jarkko Oikarinen

1989 > Nintendo releases the Game Boy

1991 > America Online is launched for DOS systems

1993 > Intel introduces the Pentium processor

1993 > *Wired* magazine is launched

1993 > The computer game *Doom* is released

1994 > Netscape's first Web browser becomes available

1994 > Yahoo! is founded

1995 > *Toy Story*—the first completely computer-generated full-length feature film—hits theaters

1995 > The Sony PlayStation debuts

1995 > Windows 95 is launched by Microsoft

1995 > The U.S. Military offers its Global Positioning System for military and civilian use

1996 > ICQ launches the first instant messenger with a Graphical User Interface (GUI)

1997 > The first DVD players become available

1997 > The first camera-phone is developed

1998 > Texas Instruments debuts the TI-89 calculator

1999 > WiFi becomes standardized

2001 > Microsoft releases Xbox, its first gaming console

2001 > Apple debuts the iPod

2001 > The Segway is introduced as a new means of transportation

2002 > The TV series *Firefly* premieres

2003 > MySpace is founded

2004 > Facebook launches at Harvard University

2004 > Flickr is developed

2005 > Apple releases the iPod Nano

2006 > Nintendo releases the Wii, its fifth-generation gaming console

2007 > Apple releases the iPhone

2007 > Microsoft launches the Windows Vista operating system

2008 > Google introduces Chrome, its first Web browser

2008 > The Large Hadron Collider successfully completes its first major test

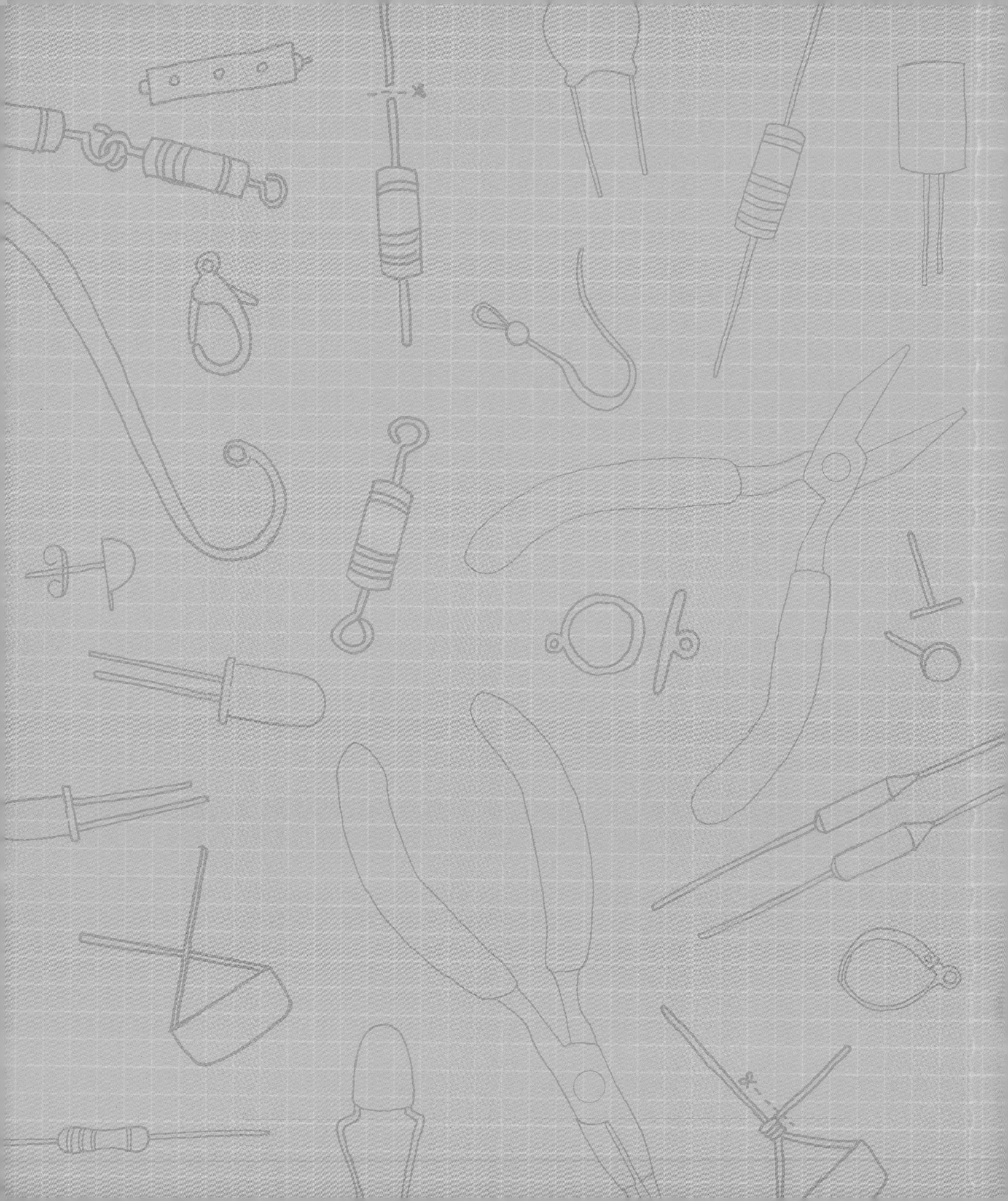

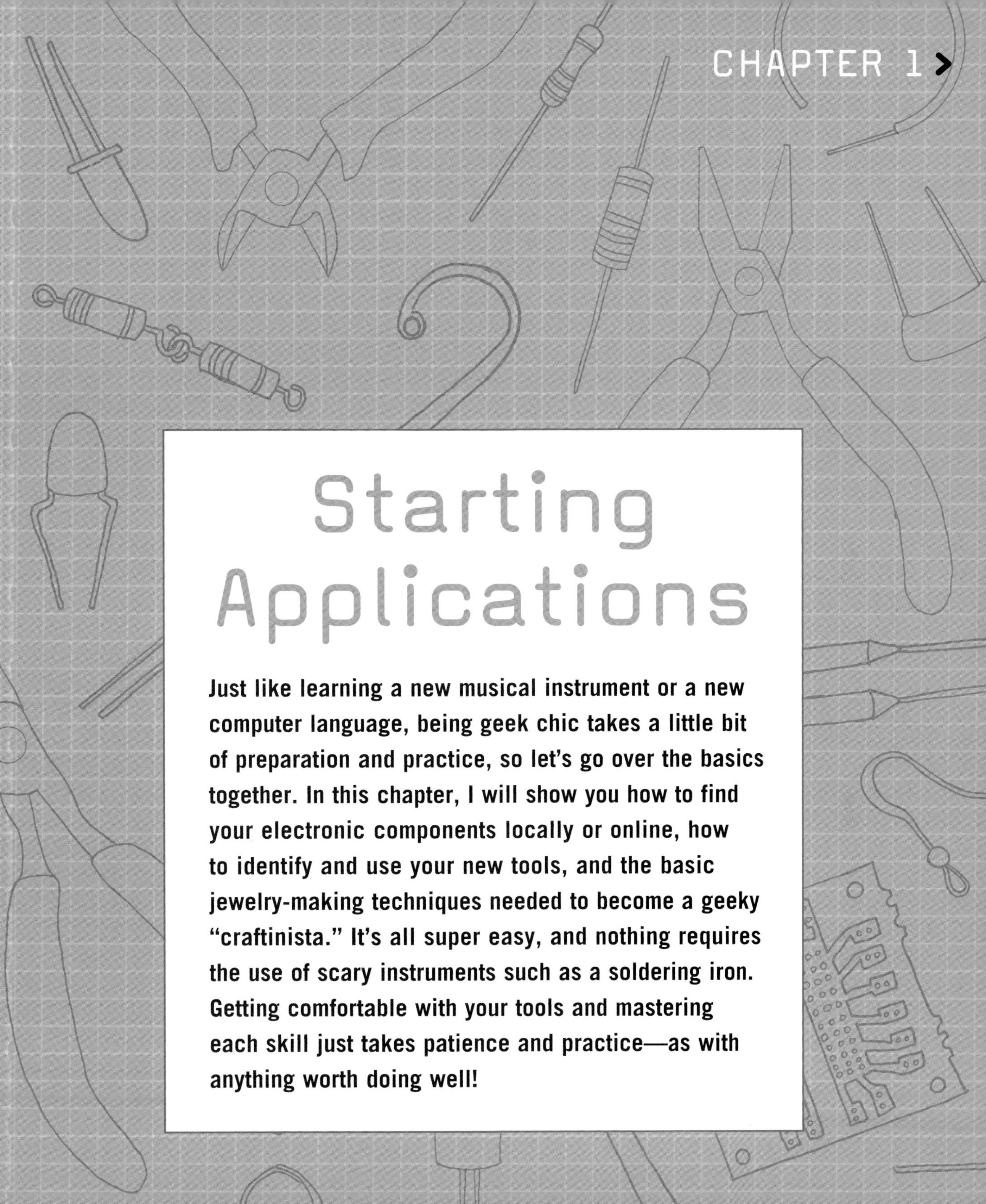

CHAPTER 1 >

Starting Applications

Just like learning a new musical instrument or a new computer language, being geek chic takes a little bit of preparation and practice, so let's go over the basics together. In this chapter, I will show you how to find your electronic components locally or online, how to identify and use your new tools, and the basic jewelry-making techniques needed to become a geeky "craftinista." It's all super easy, and nothing requires the use of scary instruments such as a soldering iron. Getting comfortable with your tools and mastering each skill just takes patience and practice—as with anything worth doing well!

COMPONENTS

I know what you're thinking: "Computer parts?! What is she talking about?" But the components used in this book aren't complicated or hard to find at all. Here's a breakdown of what you'll need and where to get it.

Hardware

All of the projects are made with just a few common electrical components.

RESISTOR > A resistor is a component that "resists" an electric current by producing a voltage drop between its "**leads**" (the wires sticking out from each end). It is most commonly used in electrical circuits in devices such as cell phones and TVs. You can usually tell a resistor by the lead on each end and the small cylinder (called the "**body**") in the middle. Other types of resistors include potentiometers (a volume-related device), varistors (a voltage-related device), and thermistors (a temperature-related device).

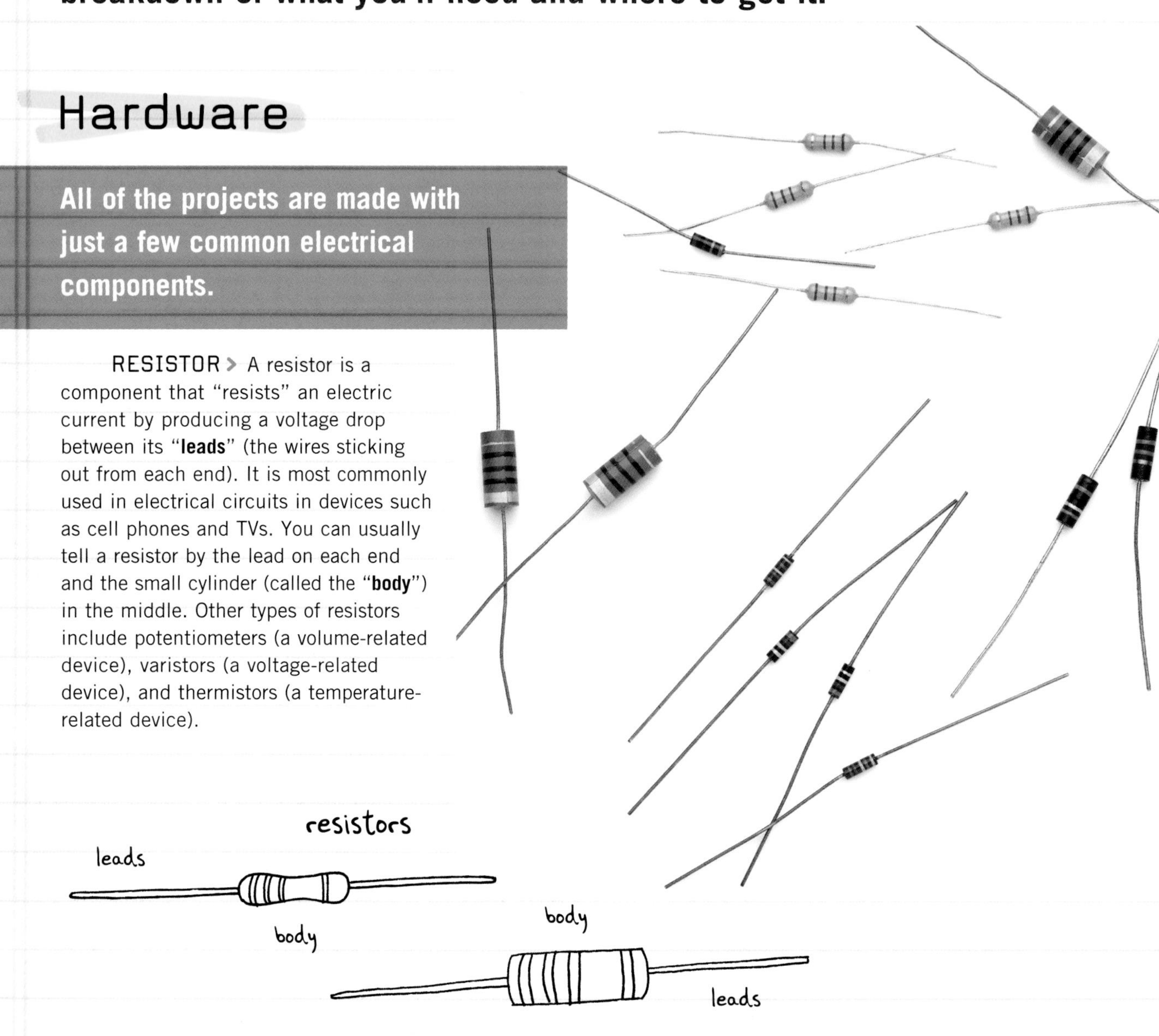

CAPACITOR > A capacitor is a device that stores energy in the electronic field between its two leads and is used on circuit boards in almost every electronic device you own. A capacitor has a central piece called a "**body**," with two **leads**, or wires, sticking out on one side (kinda like legs). Some capacitors look like resistors, but you can tell them apart because *all* capacitors have their voltage written on the side of the body, and usually in arrowlike shapes. Capacitors range greatly in size and shape—they can be square, rectangular, disk-shaped, circular, flat, chunky—and come in almost every color of the rainbow. Other types of capacitors include ceramic, mica, paper, glass, and metalized film.

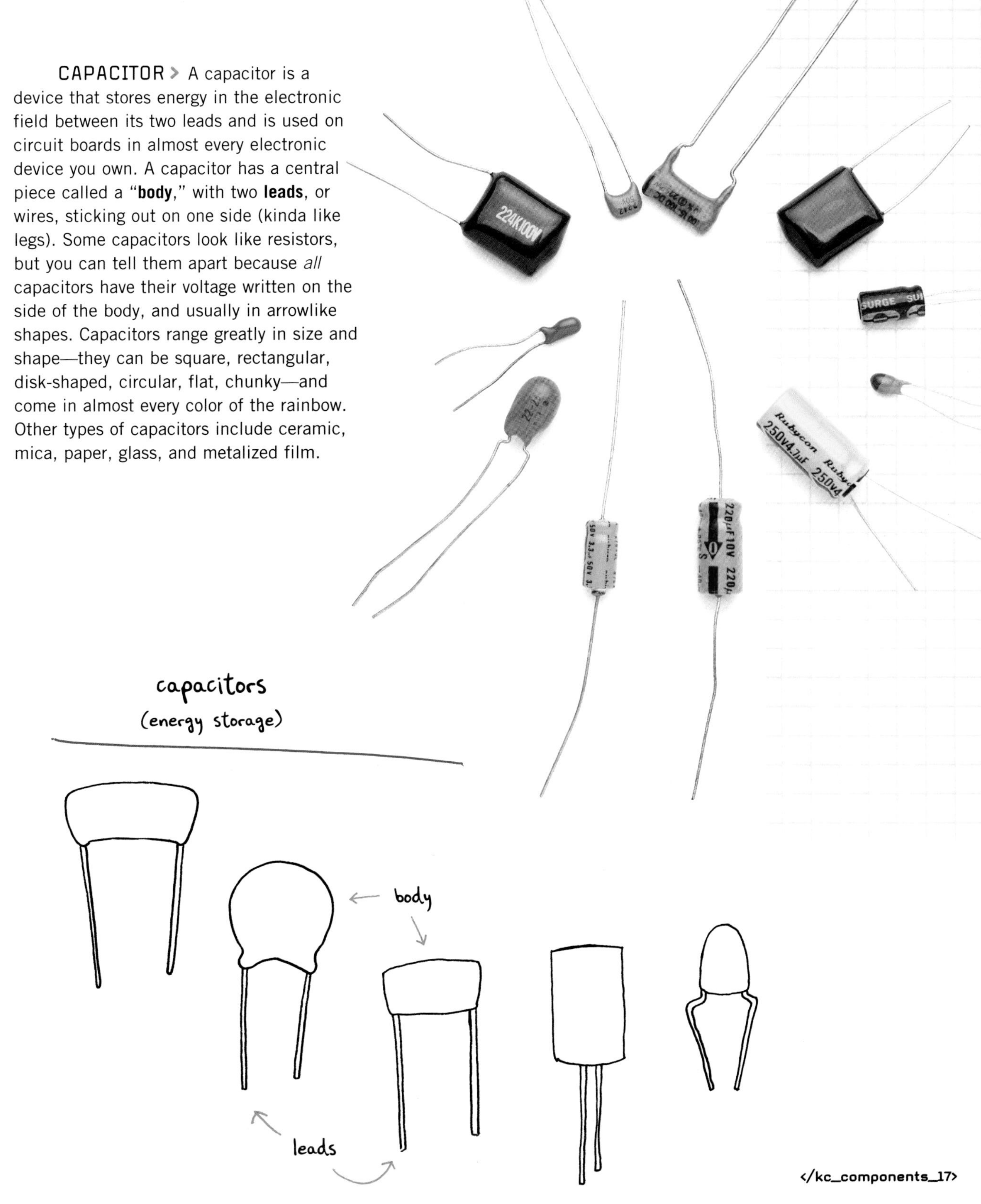

LED > A light-emitting diode (LED) emits a narrow spectrum of light. You can find LEDs in anything from flashlights to toys. The LED has a "**diode**" instead of a body and two thick, flat **leads** extending from the flat side of the diode. LEDs are just tiny lightbulbs that fit easily into an electrical circuit.

THERMAL FUSES > Thermal fuses are commonly used to keep electronics and appliances from overheating or starting a fire. Their main function is to act as safety devices to cut off or disconnect the flow of electricity should the electronic components malfunction. They come in an assortment of sizes.

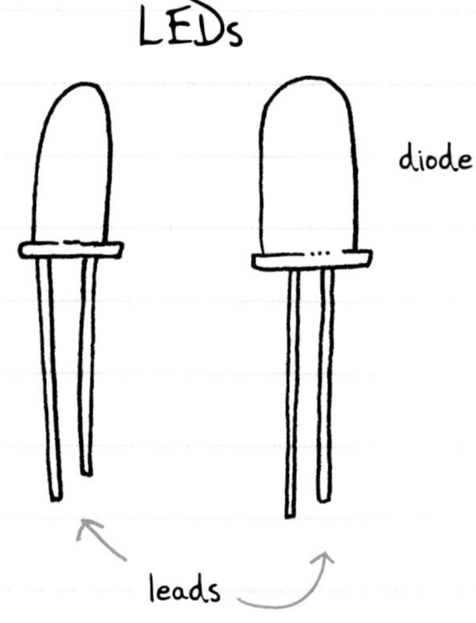

thermal fuses

I used silver thermal fuses in the Dandy Data Drop earrings on p. 36

PC BOARD > PC boards (which stands for "printed circuit boards") are the foundations of most electronic devices. They are like a blueprint, with a picture on top showing where all the resistors, capacitors, and other things are to be placed. You can find PC boards in cell phones, TVs, computers—pretty much any electronic device you come across in daily life.

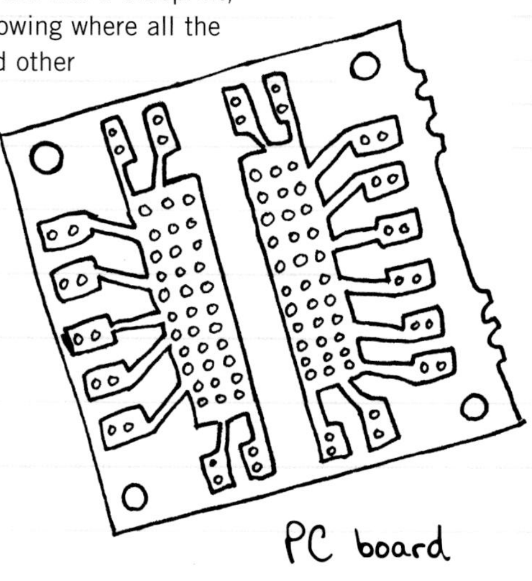

PC board

A NOTE ON SAFETY

Before you start splitting open your twenty-year-old VCR on a quest for parts—**STOP!** The parts in there have been soldered and contain lead—they are definitely hazardous. Better to stick with new or unused vintage parts instead, which are safe to use as long as you, a child, or a pet doesn't ingest them. To stay free from harm, make sure they don't end up inside or piercing your body. (This is why the earrings in this book are made with jewelry earwires as opposed to the wire from the components.) If you have curious pets or small children around, you might want to use only RoHS (Restriction of Hazardous Substances Directive)–compliant components. "RoHS–compliant" means that only an extremely limited amount of certain metals and chemicals is allowed in the piece. A few of the more exotic pieces in this book come in only non-RoHS–compliant varieties, but the vast majority are RoHS–compliant. Feel free to substitute RoHS–compliant pieces for any of the noncompliant pieces in this book.

So where do you find components such as these? Most likely, right in your hometown. Here are the best places to get them.

- **RADIO SHACK** One of the easiest places to find components is your local Radio Shack store. Just ask the sales associate to point you in the direction of the capacitors and resistors. You will find a large gray cabinet—don't be afraid to rummage around to find the perfect components.

- **THE INTERNET** The easiest place to find components is online, where you can be sure you'll locate the exact parts you need. Allied Electronics (www.alliedelec.com) and Radio Shack (www.radioshack.com) both have easy-to-search websites. Just type in the part number(s) listed in the project, and the exact pieces should pop up. Huzzah! You are in business. The hardest part about this method is the waiting. Who wants to wait for packages to come in the mail? It's all about instant gratification.

- **YOUR LOCAL COLLEGE OR UNIVERSITY** Seek out the computer or electrical engineering department and ask if they have any unused stock. It's a great way for them to get rid of old, outdated components that are taking up space. Also, it's an amazing way for you to get free parts—and even better if you get to pick and choose what you take!

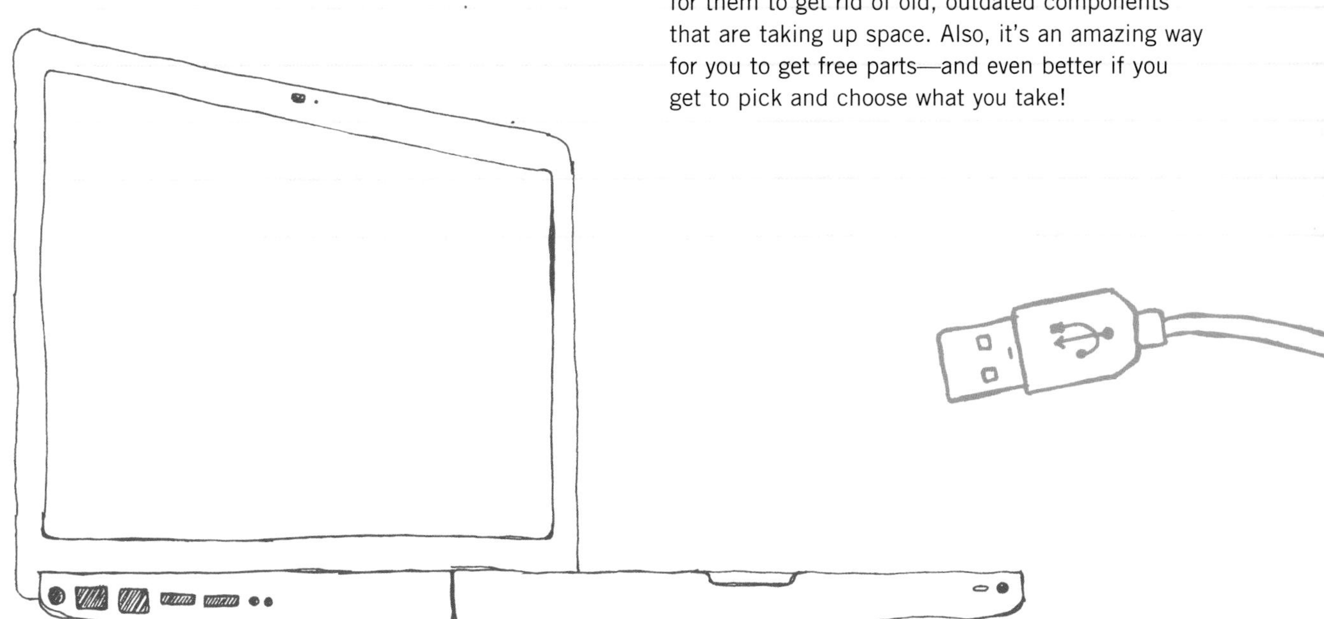

Tools

The right tools are essential for making your pieces look as professional as possible. If you think you might be doing quite a few of these projects, invest in some good tools. When I first started, I got a three-in-one tool from Wal-Mart that combines round-nose pliers, needle-nose pliers, and wire cutters in one. It worked nicely for a while, but eventually I went to a local craft store and invested in new, individual tools for each purpose. I have never looked back.

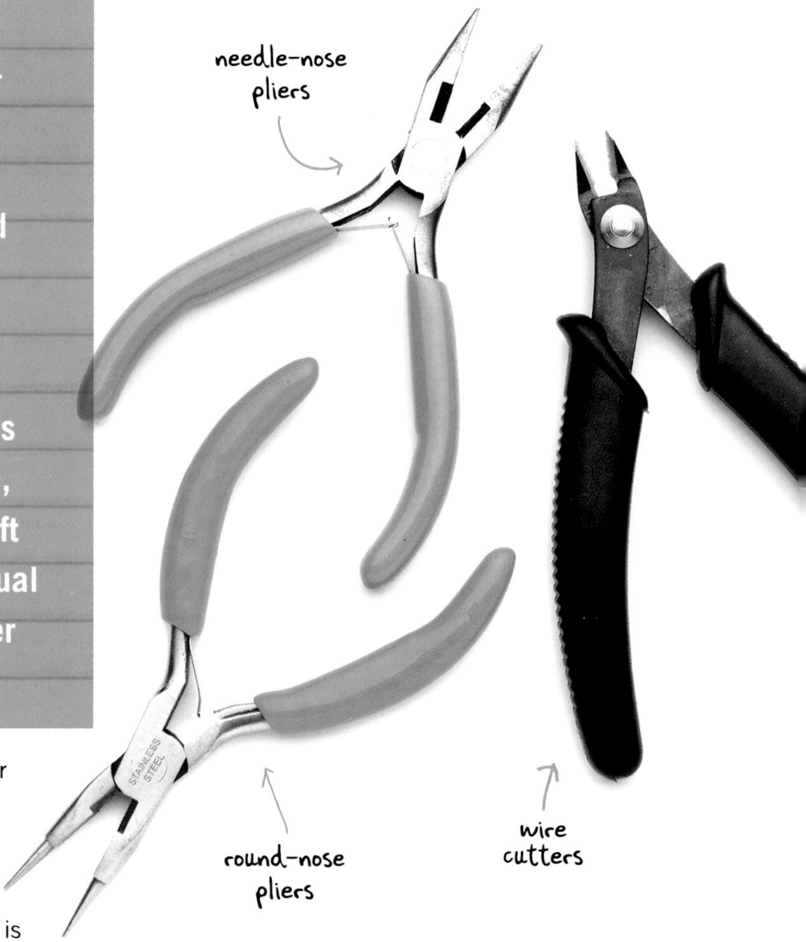

needle-nose pliers

round-nose pliers

wire cutters

You can find jewelry tools at large craft stores or online. You can even try the hardware store for needle-nose pliers or wire clippers; the round-nose pliers are specific to jewelry making. The three must-have tools listed below are used in every project in the book, so a good set of tools is essential.

ROUND-NOSE PLIERS > These are special jewelry-making pliers that help you round the ends of wires into perfect little loops, which can then be used to hang or connect other pieces.

NEEDLE-NOSE PLIERS > These pliers have pointed ends. I use them to hold leads and wires while I perform the capacitor wrap (see page 26) and to straighten out leads and wires after I make a mistake. I don't use them a lot, but they are handy when a mishap occurs or I need to hold a small part. You can use tweezers in a pinch, but I wouldn't recommend using them as your primary tool because the point is too fine to get a good grip.

WIRE CUTTERS > This tool, along with the round-nose pliers, will comprise the super-duo of your jewelry-making tool kit. They're used to closely cut and trim leads and wire. I used to just use the cutter that came on my round-nose pliers, but then I bought this and noticed a dramatic difference!

Jewelry Findings

Jewelry findings are little hoops, connectors, and clasps that enable you to wear what you've made. You can find them at local craft stores, chain stores, and online merchants.

EARRING CLOSURES > This is what you attach to a piece to turn it into an earring and thread it through your earlobe. There are many different types: French, lever-back, half-ball studs, hoops, and regular stud earrings, to name a few. I prefer plain French or hooklike earwires, but feel free to substitute any type that is comfortable to you. Note that clutches (earring backs) usually have to be bought separately.

PIN BACKS > There are two main types of pin backs: the locking-bar pin back and the dot pin back. I prefer the dot pin back because it works with smaller pieces. As with the earring backs, make sure to purchase the clutches, as most jewelry websites have them listed separately. I have used the locking-bar pin backs before and got frustrated at how large they were; however, they are a lot easier to find.

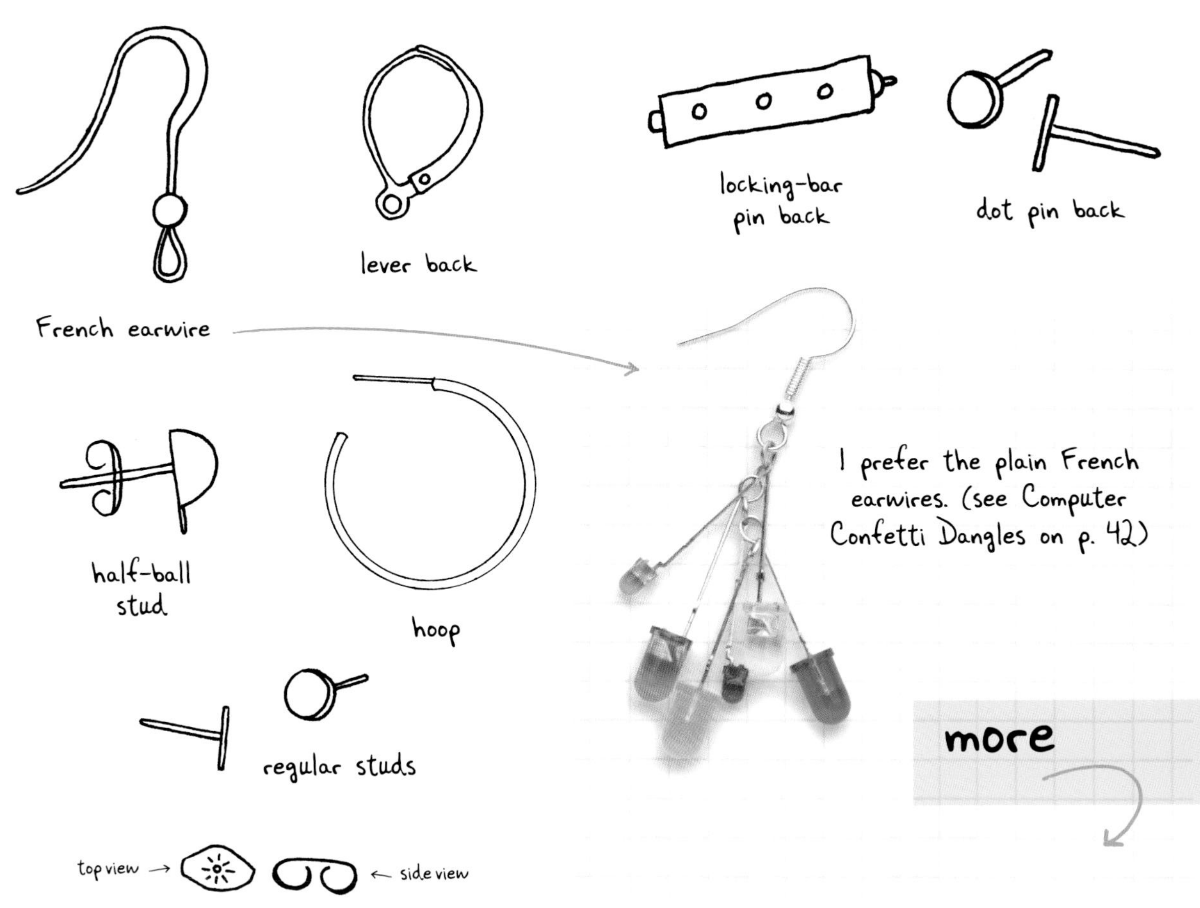

more

NECKLACE/BRACELET CLASPS > There is an overwhelming variety of necklace and bracelet clasps available: lobster, magnetic, s-lock, ball and joint . . . it's hard to choose! After much trial and error, I discovered that I prefer the toggle clasp because it looks classy, is versatile, and is easy to put on. Feel free to use whichever type of clasp works best for you in any of the neckware or wristware projects.

JEWELRY WIRE > Jewelry wire comes in a variety of "gauges" (or thicknesses) and materials. When it comes to gauge, the smaller the number, the heavier the wire; for example, 16-gauge wire is thicker than 20-gauge wire. The most common gauges are 16, 18, and 20. Wire also comes in many materials, including gold, silver, brass, sterling, copper, and coated colored wire. Feel free to use any type or gauge of wire you desire for the projects in this book.

JUMP RINGS AND SPRING RINGS > These are little metal circles used to connect jewelry pieces. A jump ring is a solid metal circle, while a spring ring looks like a tiny key ring. Be sure to check out the tutorial on page 27 for the correct way to open and close a jump ring.

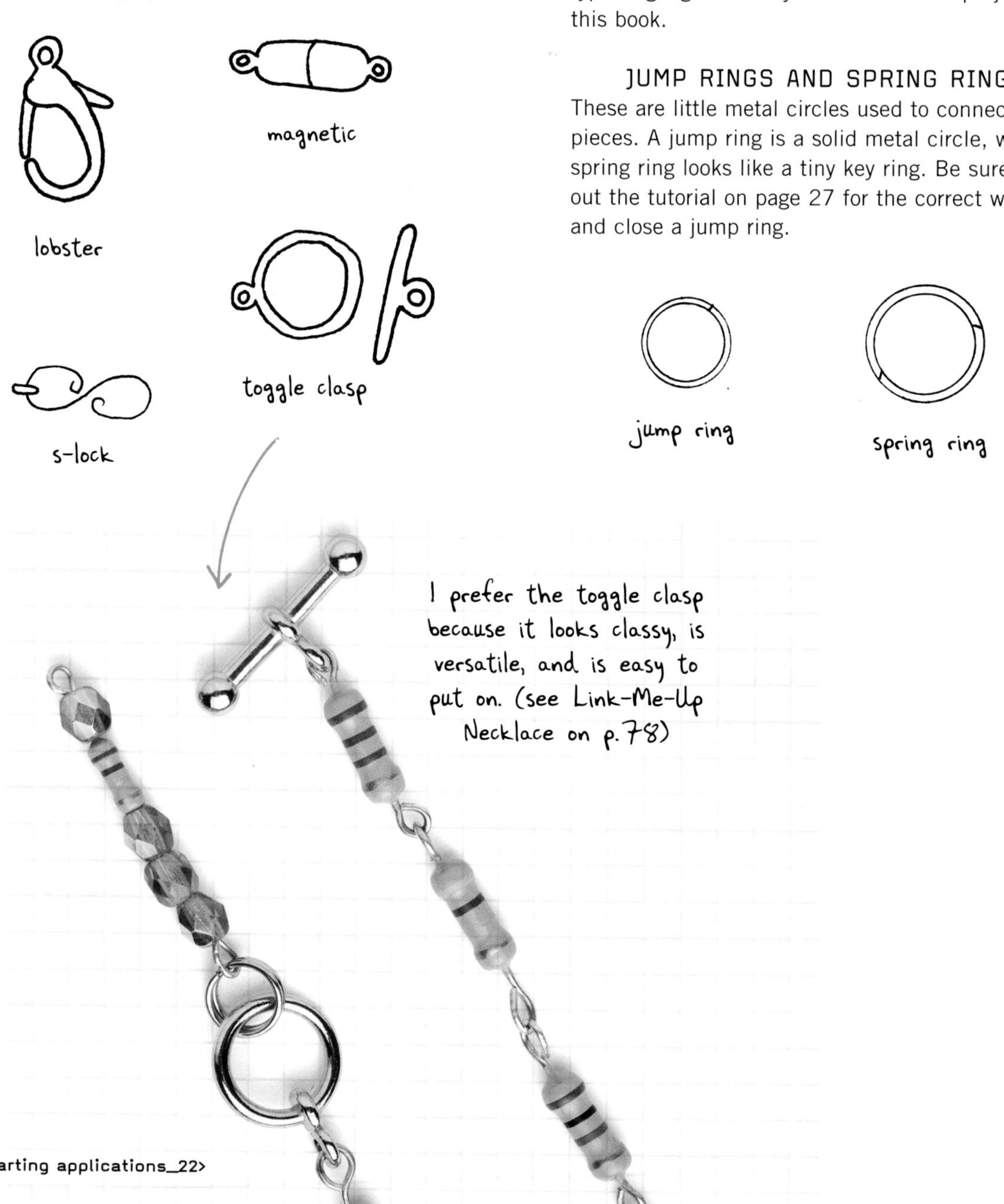

OTHER FINDINGS > Some additional findings appear only once or twice in the book. You can find all of these at local craft stores or online jewelry-crafting merchants.

- **Bangle** is a common term for a plain metal bracelet. Sometimes bangles have a closure; other times they are just plain metal rings.
- **Bracelet frames** are basically cuffs that you can wrap wire around to customize your own bracelet.
- **Rings with loops** are exactly what they sound like: ring bases with tiny loops to which you can attach your beads or components.

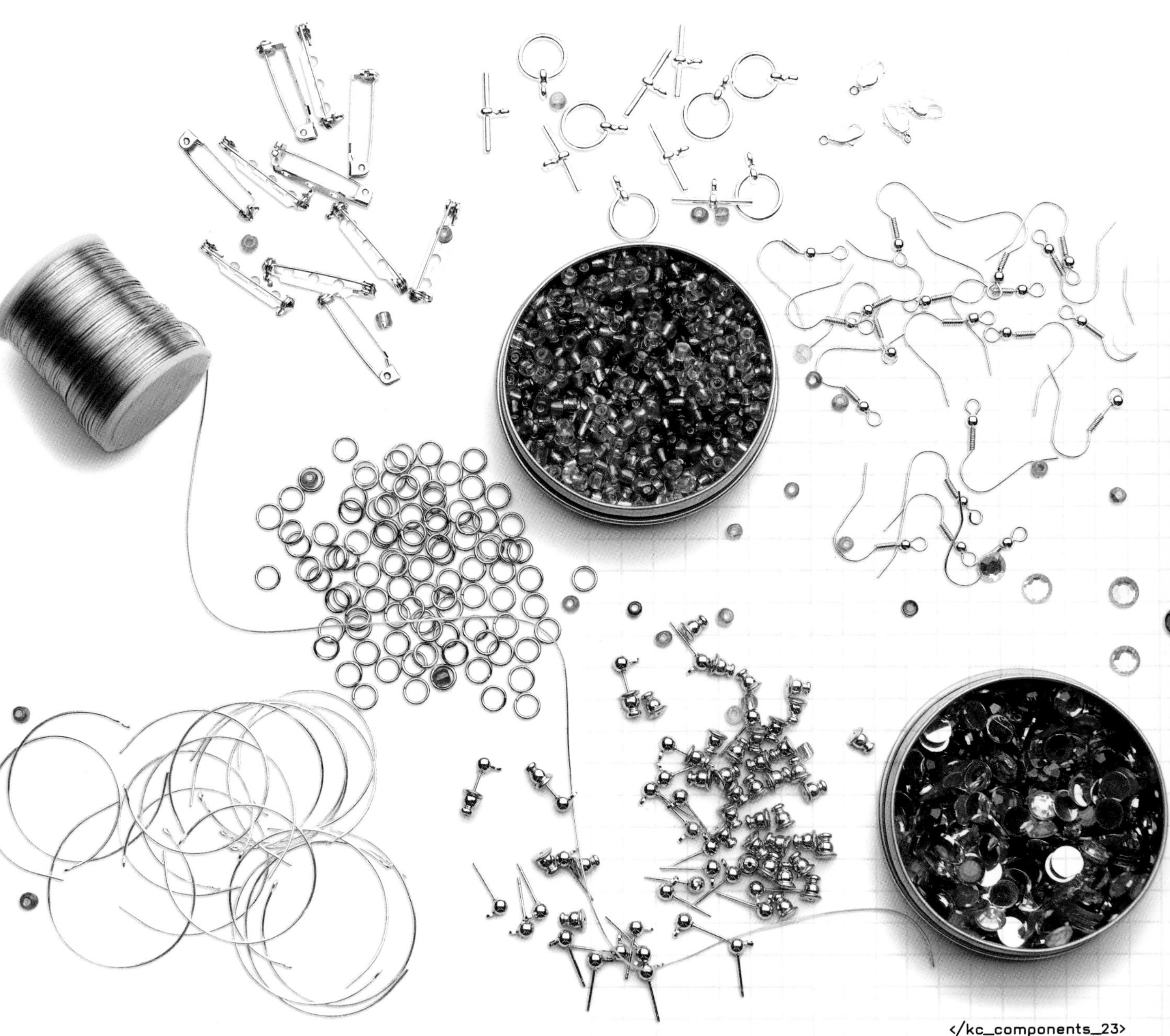

BASIC TECHNOLOGY

There are a few techniques that are essential to completing most of the projects. They may seem a little complicated at first, but once you get the hang of them they're as easy as riding a bike. If you are nervous about messing up a project because it's a gift for a friend or something special for yourself, just buy extra parts and practice, practice, practice.

Looping a Lead

Making little loops on the ends of the leads is probably the skill you will use the most for the projects in this book—and it's super easy! These loops make it possible to attach all the pieces together.

1. Hold round-nose pliers in your dominant hand and a resistor in your other hand.

2. Use the pliers to grip the very end of the wire. Begin to roll the round-nose pliers toward the center of the resistor until you make a complete circle.

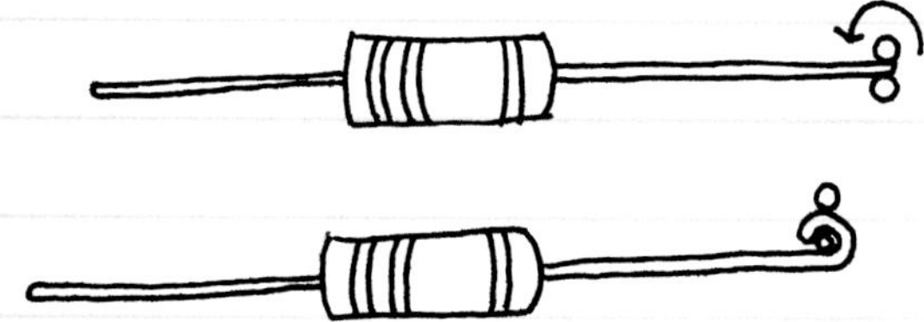

3. Where the two wires meet, grip the main wire right under that and bend the wire slightly to make the loop symmetrical at the end.

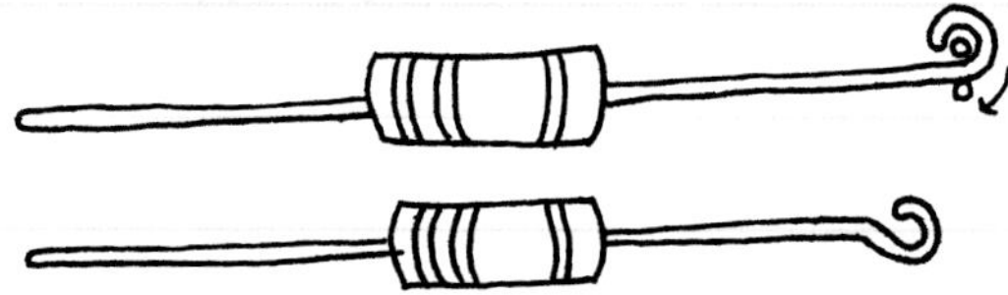

4. Use needle-nose pliers to squeeze the loop shut.

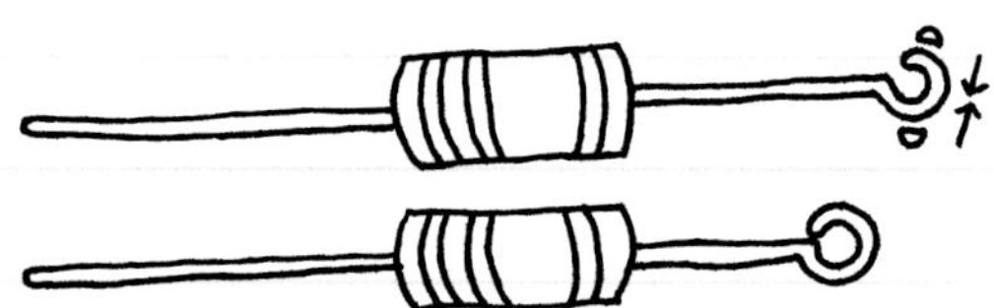

Making a Resistor Chain

Many projects ask you to connect several resistors end to end to form a chain. Here's how to do it.

1. Take a resistor and trim both leads to a little less than ½ inch (1.3 cm).

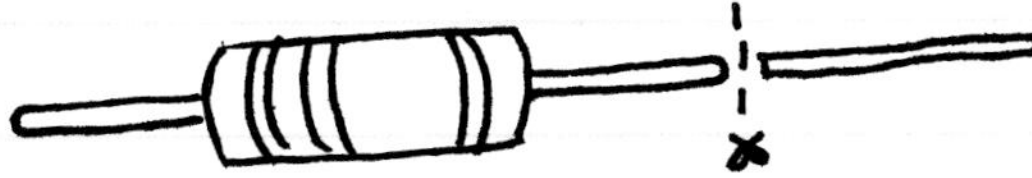

2. Use round-nose pliers to loop the end of each lead (see "Looping a Lead," left). The larger the loop, the smoother the resistor chain will lay without tangling or kinking. I do like the look of smaller loops, though, so I try to find a happy medium.

3. Grip the base of each loop next to the body of the resistor with round-nose pliers and straighten until it is symmetrical.

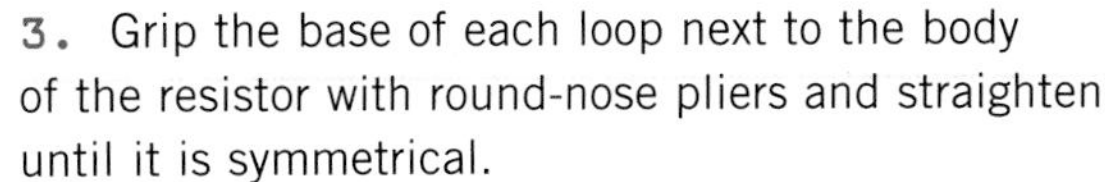

4. Attach the loops to each other to form a chain.

5. Use needle-nose pliers to squeeze both loops closed.

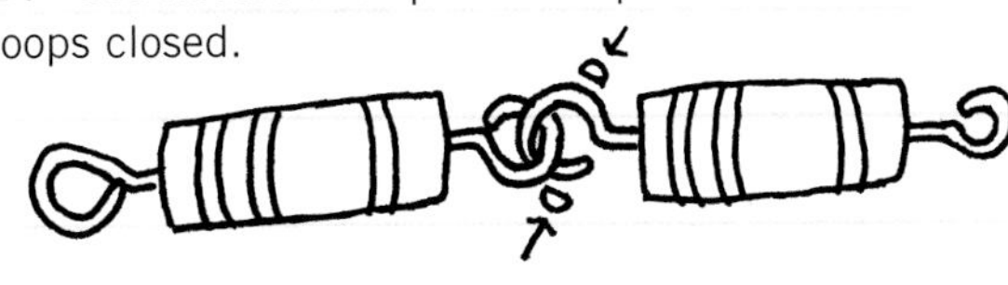

6. Repeat steps 1–5 with as many resistors as you want in the chain.

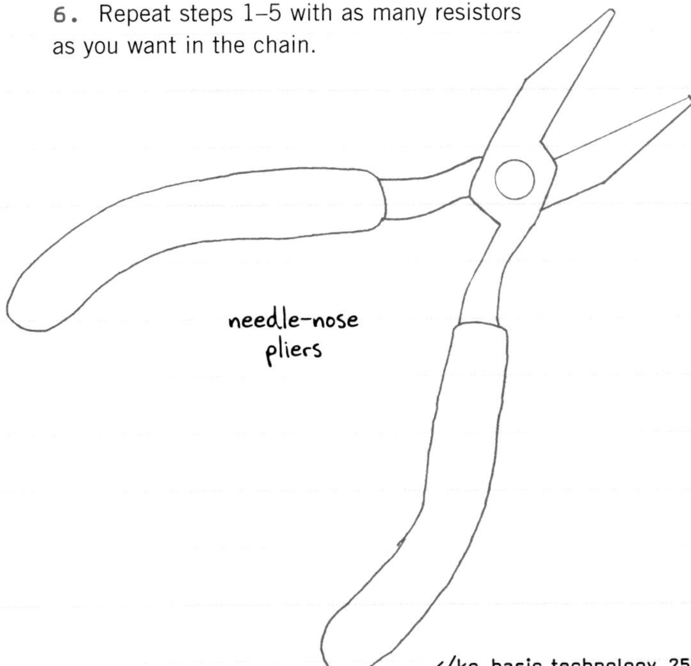

Doing a Capacitor Wrap

This is another commonly used technique, used to join the two leads on a capacitor and wrap them together to form one loop.

1. Take a capacitor and hold it with the body at the bottom, making a U shape.

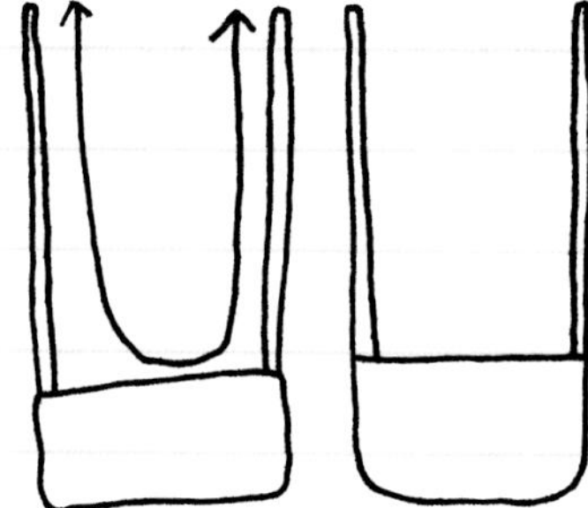

2. Use your fingers to cross the leads, making an X.

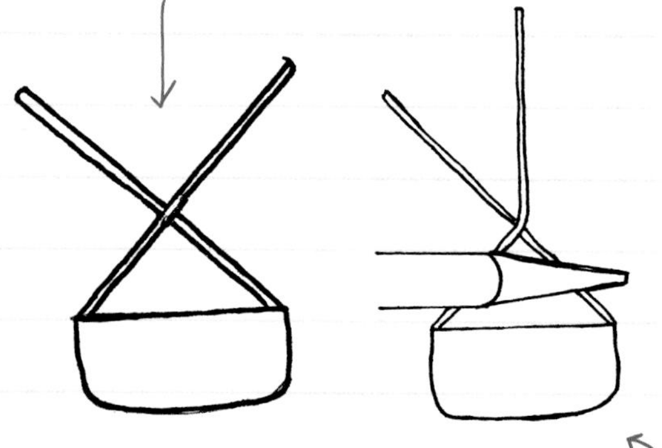

3. Use needle-nose pliers to grip the leads beneath the intersection of the X, holding them steady. Then take round-nose pliers and bend one lead straight up from where the X intersects.

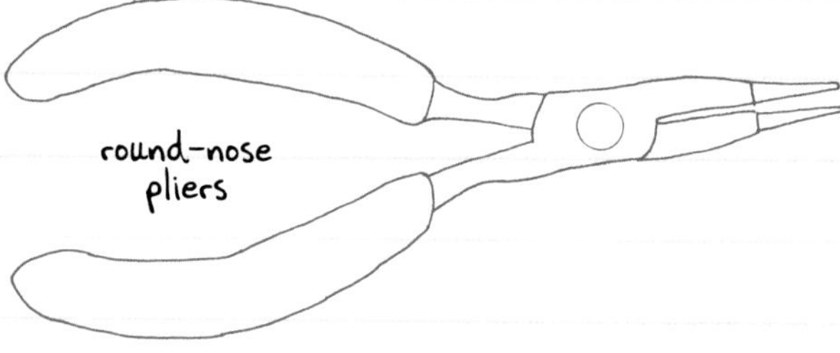

4. Grip the capacitor with needle-nose pliers to keep it steady and use your fingers to wrap the bent lead around the straight lead two to three times.

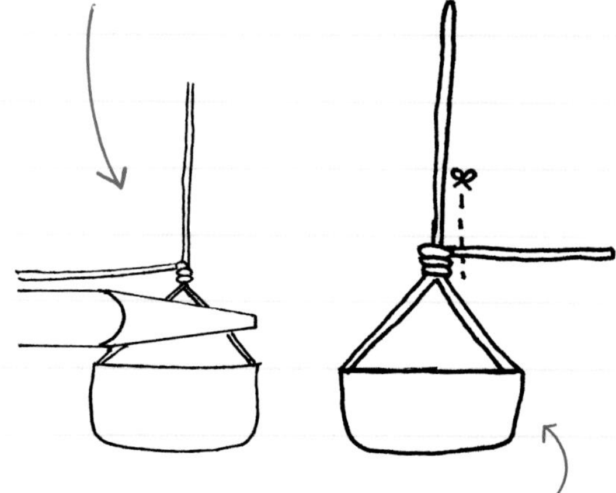

5. Trim the excess wire with wire clippers.

6. Straighten the remaining lead with needle-nose pliers. Trim the lead to ½ inch (1.3 cm) with wire clippers.

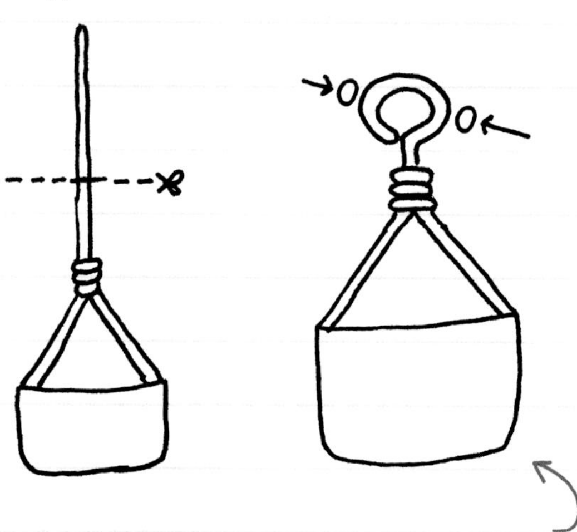

7. Use round-nose pliers to loop the end of the trimmed lead (see "Looping a Lead" on page 24).

Adding Jump Rings

Jump rings are useful for several applications, but mainly I use them to contain many components on one large ring. It's important to open and close the rings gently so that you don't distort or even break the ring.

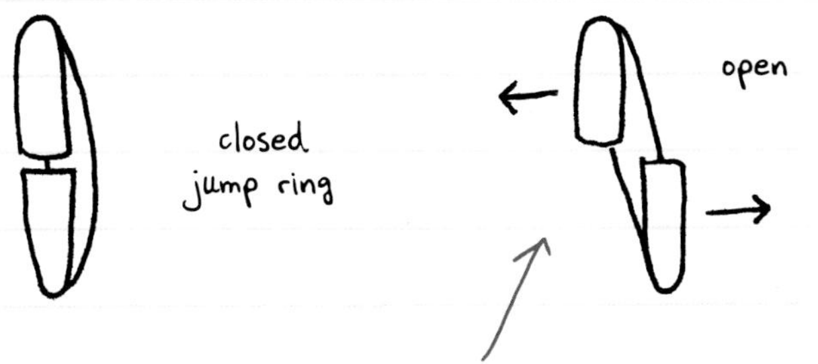

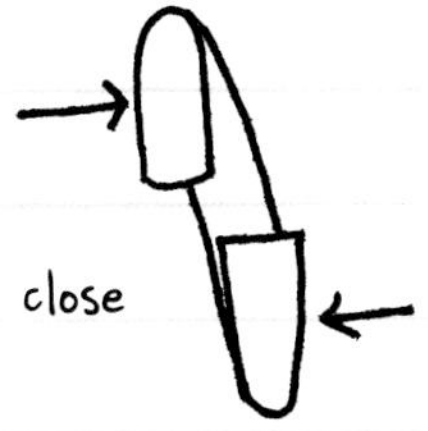

1. Take needle-nose pliers and a jump ring. Use the pliers to open the jump ring horizontally. Slide or attach a component onto the jump ring.

2. Push the ring back together with your needle-nose pliers to close it.

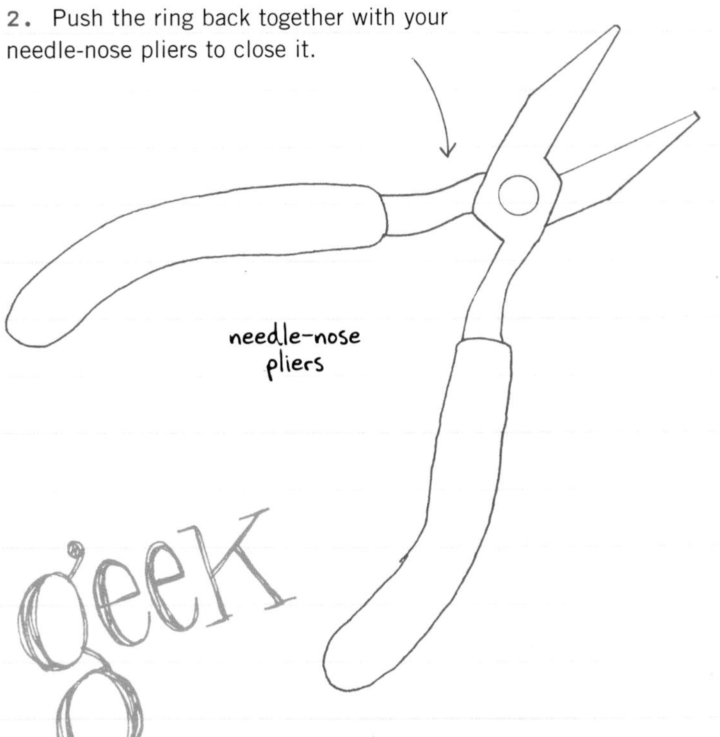

GEEK SPEAK

LOL > laugh out loud

BRB > be right back

OMG > oh my goodness

OIC > oh, I see

Bookmark > save for later: "That dress is so cute, I am going to have to bookmark it!"

Woot! > an exclamation of happiness: "I just got an A+ on my test! Woot!"

1337 > sometimes also l33t or leet, meaning "elite"

kthxbye > okay, thanks, goodbye

ORLY > oh, really?

WYSIWYG > what you see is what you get

Web 2.0 > socially driven Web content

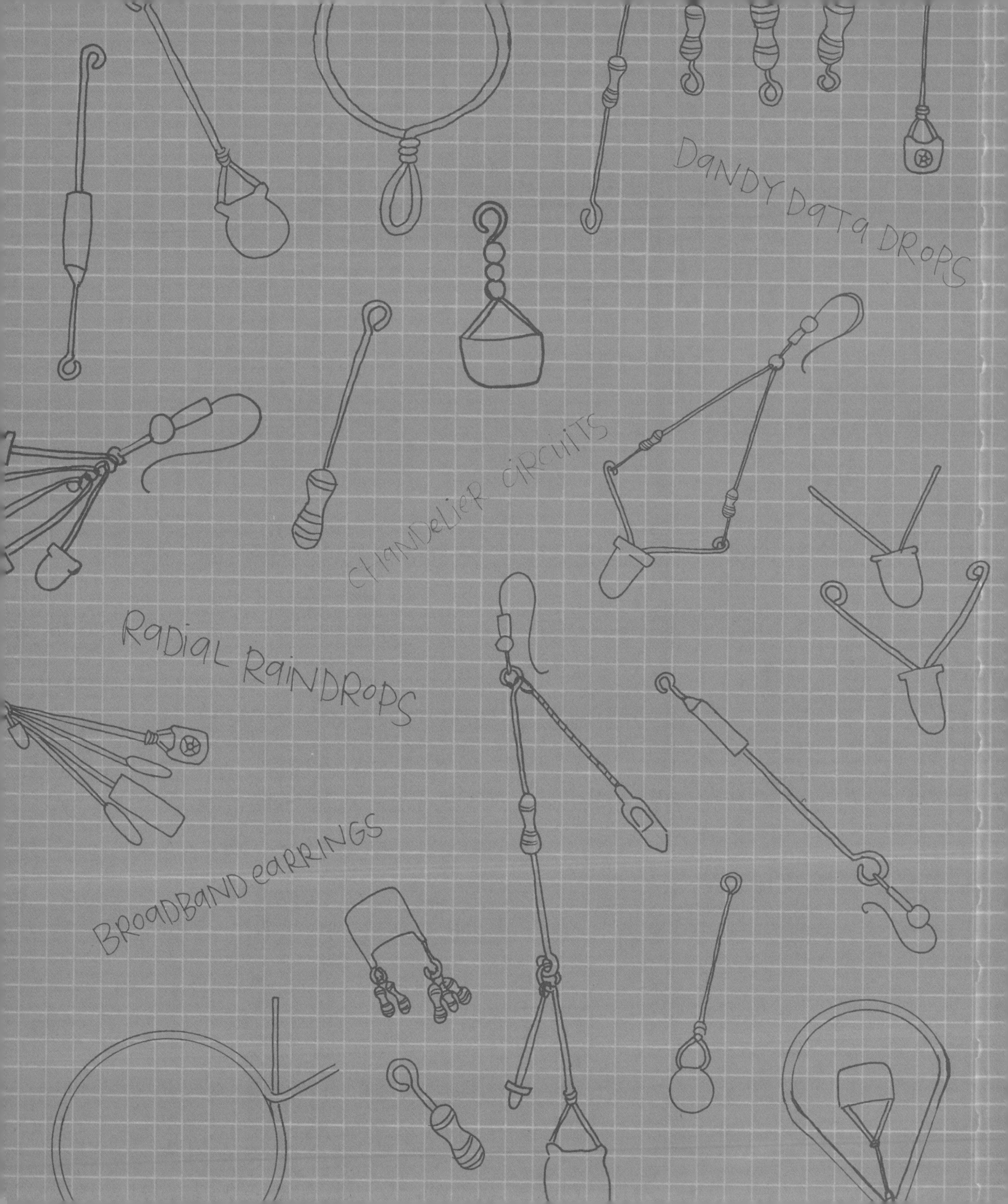
DanDY Data DRoPS
CHanDeLieR CiRCuiTS
RaDiaL RaiNDRoPS
BRoaDBAND eaRRINGS

CHAPTER 2 >

Earware

Ready to dive in? Let's start with some eclectic—and electric—earrings, which are a staple of my accessories wardrobe and a great way to integrate a little geekiness into your style. These 12 projects start pretty simple and progress in difficulty as you move through the chapter; try them all and you'll be amazed at how quickly your skills and technique develop. Don't hesitate to customize your projects and make them your very own, either by following the "Customize Your App" suggestions in each project or brainstorming your own variations—that's the geek chic way!

{easy}

Technicolor Magic

These are the perfect earrings on which to practice the capacitor wrap, because you can easily cover your mistakes with beads! Simple and quick to do, these earrings also make great gifts. Pick beads that coordinate with your capacitors. I like to use bright, colorful beads with neutral-colored capacitors or more subdued, neutral beads with bright capacitors; but your taste is always your own.

COMPONENTS AND HARDWARE

- 2 MEDIUM BROWN CAPACITORS {Allied part number: 613-0546}
- 6 6/0 OR E BEAD SEED BEADS
- 2 FRENCH EARWIRES
- NEEDLE-NOSE PLIERS
- ROUND-NOSE PLIERS
- WIRE CUTTERS

application

1. Take a brown capacitor and follow steps 1 to 5 of the capacitor wrap (see page 26), stopping before you trim and loop the last lead.

2. String three beads onto the lead.

3. Trim the exposed end of the lead to about ½ inch (1.3 cm). Then use round-nose pliers to loop the end. As you make the loop, slide a French earwire onto it. Close the loop and either trim the excess wire or tuck it into the top bead.

4. Repeat for the other earring.

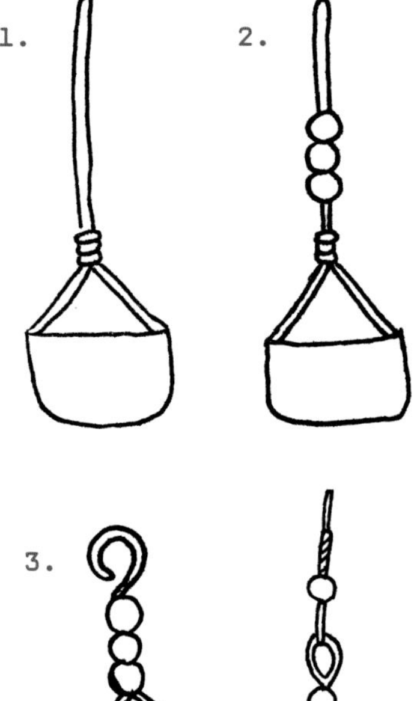

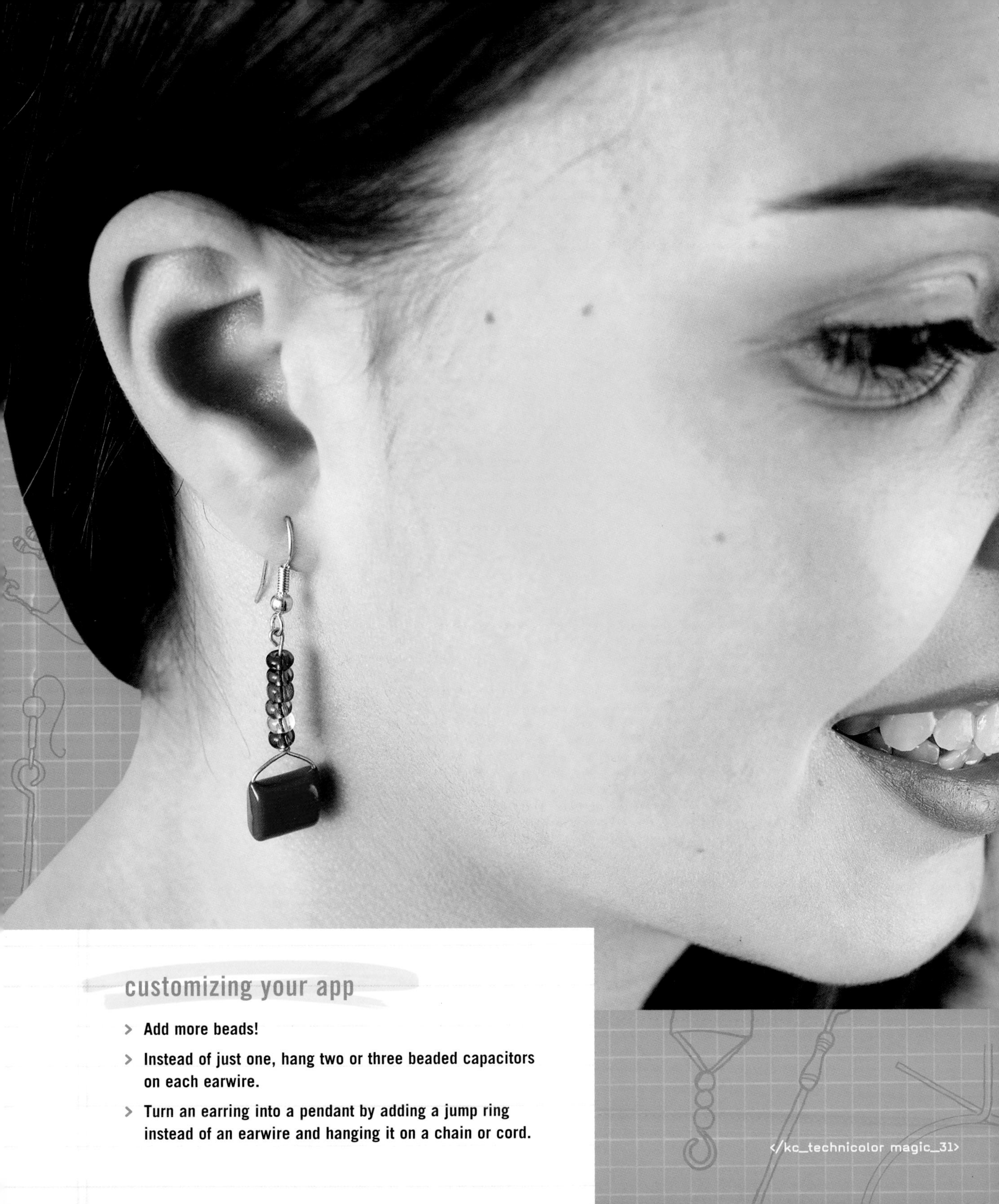

customizing your app

- Add more beads!
- Instead of just one, hang two or three beaded capacitors on each earwire.
- Turn an earring into a pendant by adding a jump ring instead of an earwire and hanging it on a chain or cord.

{easy}

Pretty Pixels

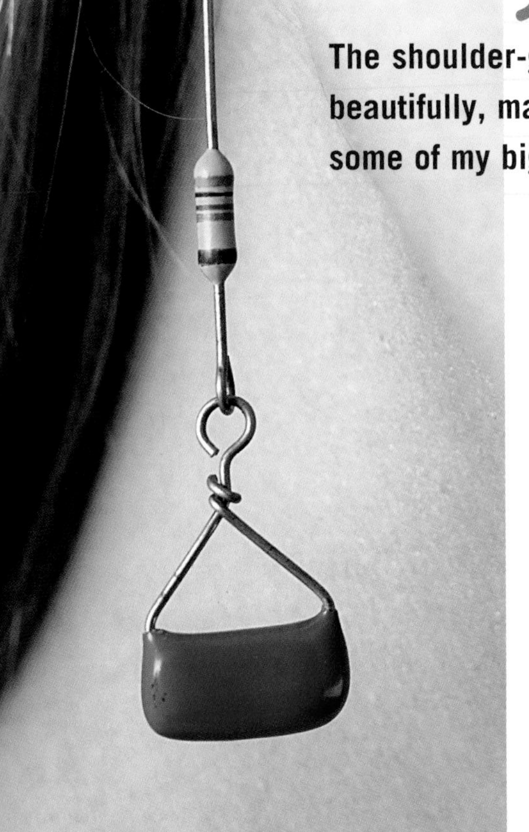

The shoulder-grazing length of these earrings elongates the neck beautifully, making you feel super graceful and elegant. These are some of my biggest sellers because of their simplicity and versatility.

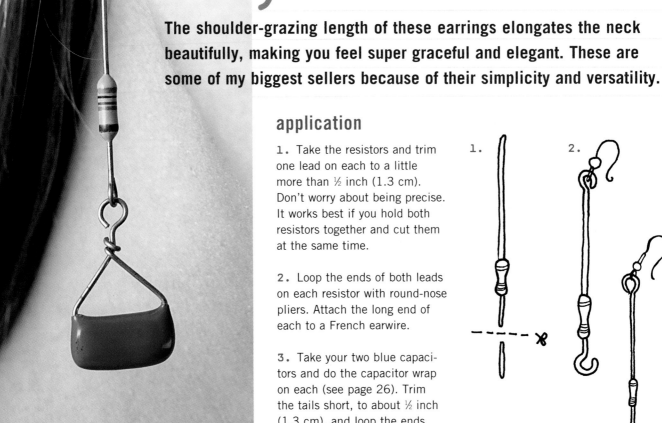

application

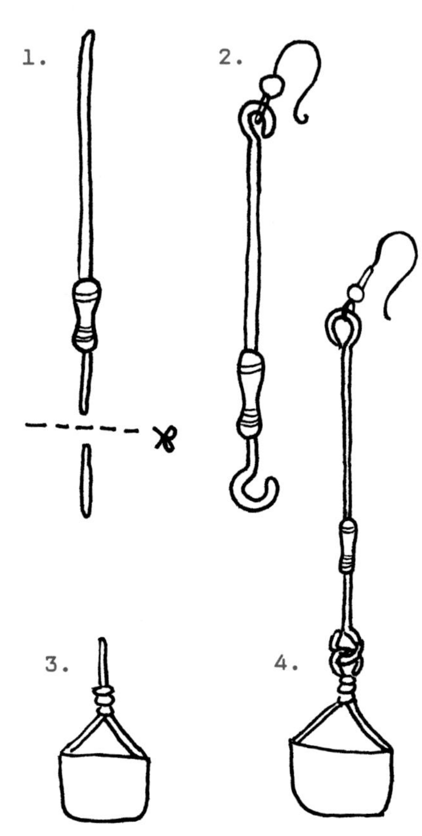

1. Take the resistors and trim one lead on each to a little more than ½ inch (1.3 cm). Don't worry about being precise. It works best if you hold both resistors together and cut them at the same time.

2. Loop the ends of both leads on each resistor with round-nose pliers. Attach the long end of each to a French earwire.

3. Take your two blue capacitors and do the capacitor wrap on each (see page 26). Trim the tails short, to about ½ inch (1.3 cm), and loop the ends with round-nose pliers.

4. Attach one looped capacitor to the short end of one resistor with round-nose pliers. Repeat for the second earring. Close all loops securely.

COMPONENTS AND HARDWARE

- 2 LONG GREEN RESISTORS {Allied part number: 648-0204}
- 2 BLUE CAPACITORS {Allied part number: 613-0555}
- 2 FRENCH EARWIRES
- NEEDLE-NOSE PLIERS
- ROUND-NOSE PLIERS
- WIRE CUTTERS

customizing your app

- **Dangle more than one capacitor from each resistor.**
- **Slide beads onto either end of the resistor.**
- **Chain together a bunch of resistors cut short, instead of using one long one.**

You can mix and match with my other designs if you have double-pierced ears.
See page 40 to learn how to make Orange You Happy Dangles.
Pretty Pixels

{easy}

LAN Party Dangles

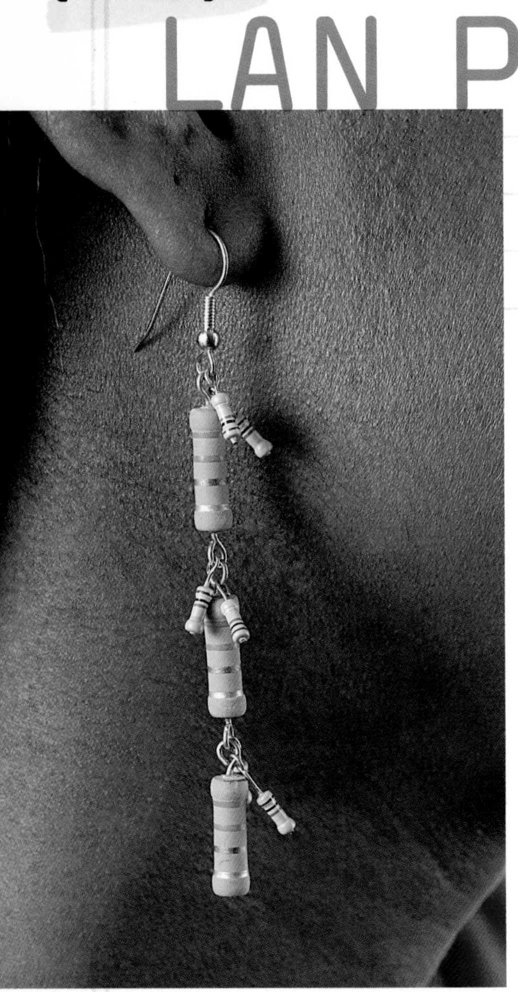

I love parties—but then, who doesn't? I wanted these earrings to capture the energy of a great party—lots of people, interesting conversation, and tons of new faces. Bright and diverse, with a lot of movement, these earrings look like the perfect party to me!

COMPONENTS AND HARDWARE

- 6 LARGE GREEN RESISTORS {Allied part number: 296-2282}
- 12 SMALL BLUE RESISTORS {Radio Shack part number: 271-309}
- 2 FRENCH EARWIRES
- NEEDLE-NOSE PLIERS
- ROUND-NOSE PLIERS
- WIRE CUTTERS

application

1. Make two resistor chains, each with three green resistors (see "Making a Resistor Chain" on page 25). The bottom resistor on each chain doesn't need an end loop—you can just cut the lead off entirely.

2. Use needle-nose pliers to attach a French earwire to the top of each chain.

3. Take the small blue resistors and trim one lead on each to a little more than ½ inch (1.3 cm). Cut off the second lead completely. Use needle-nose pliers to loop the leads.

4. Use needle-nose pliers to attach the twelve blue resistors to each chain where the large resistors are looped together. Close all loops securely.

1.

4.

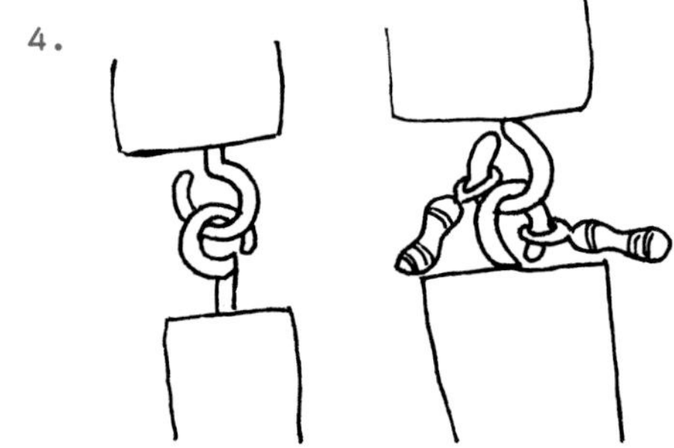

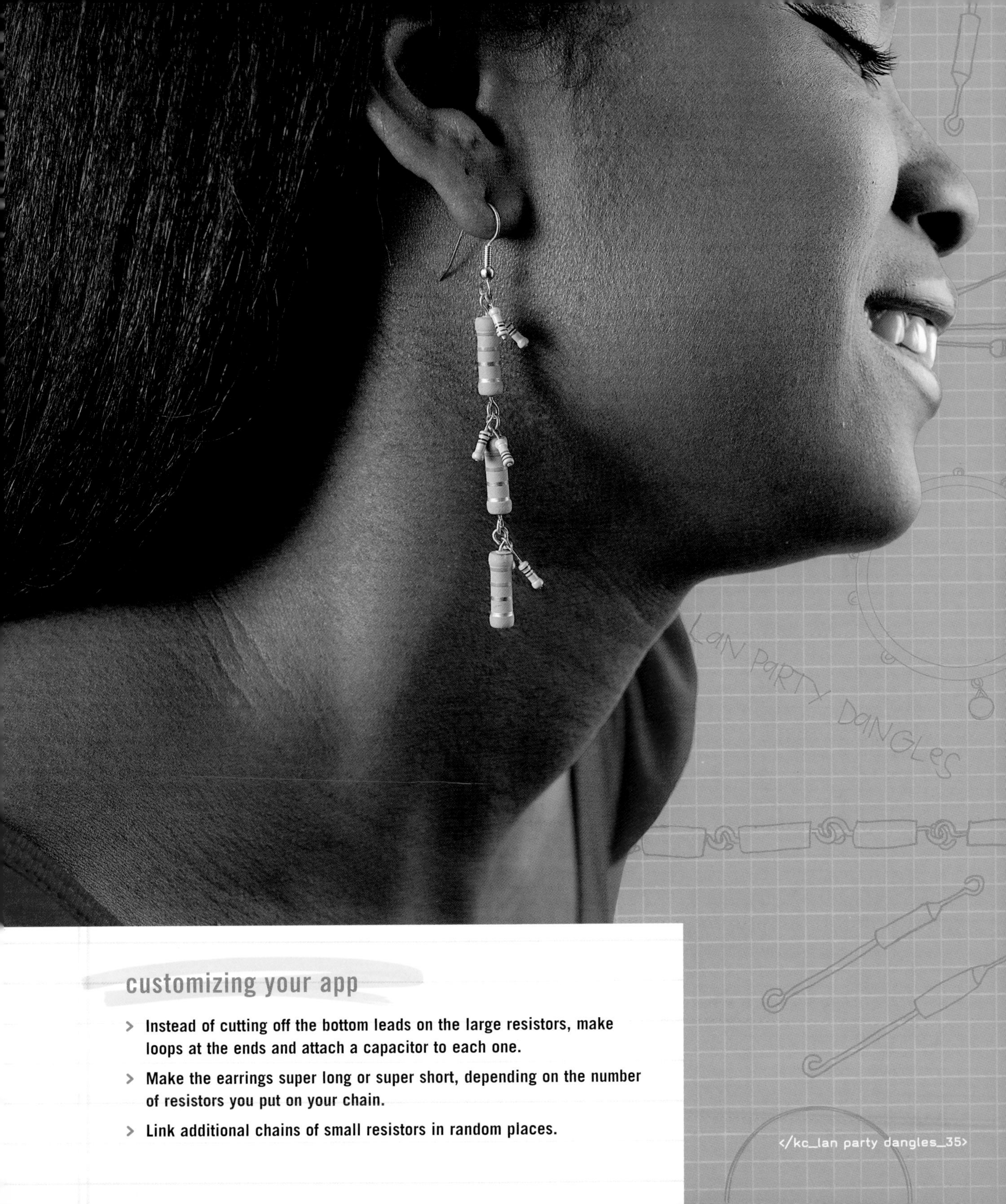

customizing your app

- Instead of cutting off the bottom leads on the large resistors, make loops at the ends and attach a capacitor to each one.
- Make the earrings super long or super short, depending on the number of resistors you put on your chain.
- Link additional chains of small resistors in random places.

{easy}

Dandy Data Drops

This is a great pair of earrings to showcase a variety of different resistors. Don't be afraid to mix it up with all kinds of crazy colors and sizes.

application

1. If you are using medium resistors, trim one lead on each to a little less than ½ inch (1.3 cm). Leave the other lead long. If you are using thermal fuses, no trimming is necessary. Loop both ends, but do not completely close the loops.

2. Attach an earwire to the long end of each thermal fuse or medium resistor. Use needle-nose pliers to squeeze the loop closed.

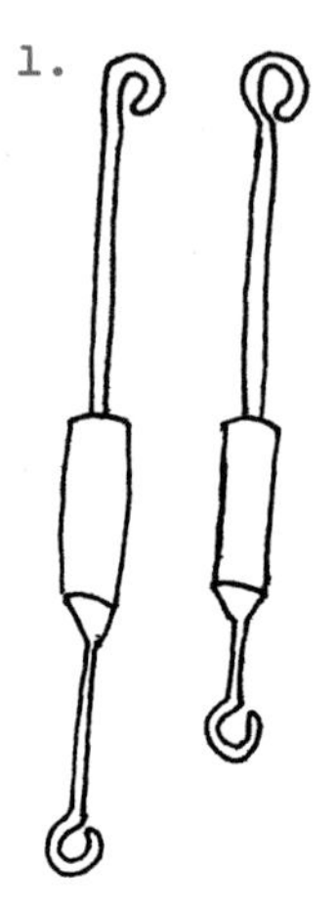

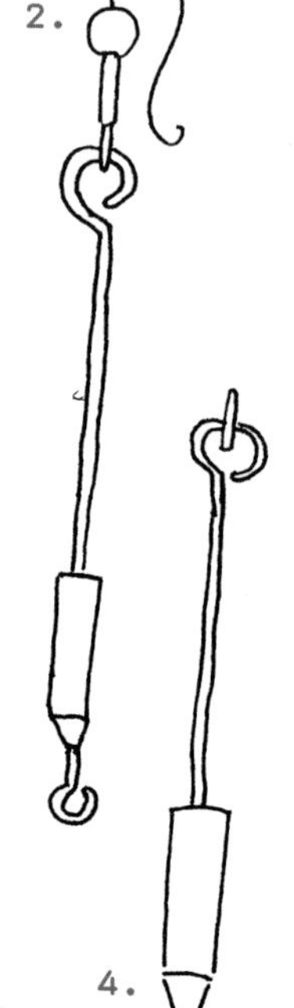

3. Take the tan resistors and cut one lead completely off each one. Trim the other leads at varying lengths. Use round-nose pliers to loop the ends.

4. Slide three small resistors onto the short end of each thermal fuse or medium resistor. Use needle-nose pliers to squeeze the loops closed.

COMPONENTS AND HARDWARE

- 2 SILVER THERMAL FUSES {Radio Shack part number: 270-1322} OR MEDIUM RESISTORS
- 6 SMALL TAN RESISTORS {Radio Shack part number: 271-308}
- 2 FRENCH EARWIRES
- NEEDLE-NOSE PLIERS
- ROUND-NOSE PLIERS
- WIRE CLIPPERS

customizing your app

- **Make the earrings shorter by trimming the leads in steps 1 and 2.**
- **Instead of hanging only three small resistors from each thermal fuse, pack it with ten or more.**
- **Replace the thermal fuse or medium resistors with a chain of resistors, then hang a bunch of small resistors from the end.**

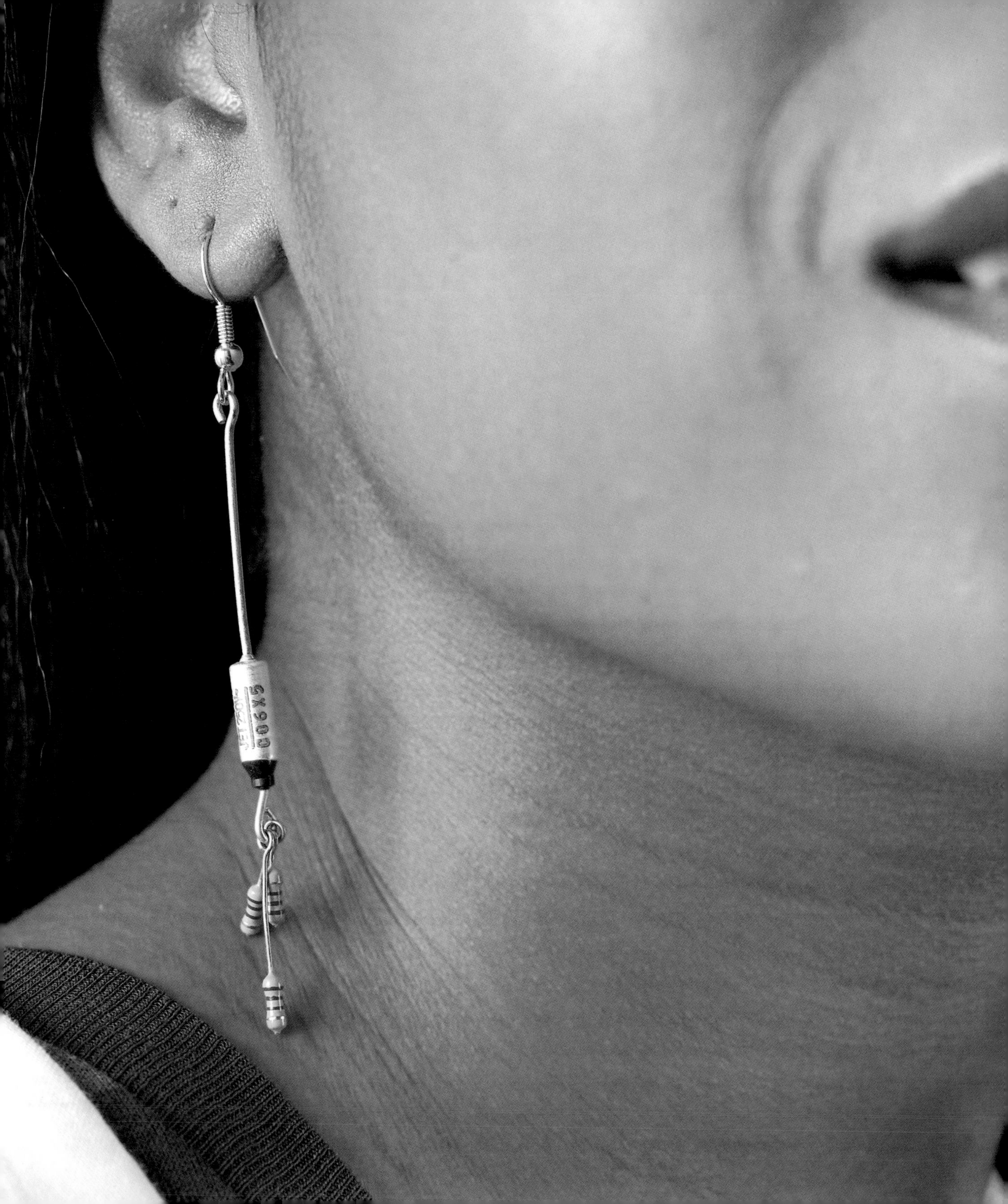
C06X5

{easy}

Little Bytes

Even as a little girl I loved having neat little things that nobody else had and making my own jewelry. This is a great project to make for your favorite young geek who's not quite ready for long, dangly earrings.

COMPONENTS AND HARDWARE

- **2 MEDIUM GREEN CAPACITORS** {Radio Shack part number: 272-1070}
- **10 SMALL TAN RESISTORS** {Radio Shack part number: 271-308}
- **2 STUD EARRING BASES AND CLUTCHES**
- **NEEDLE-NOSE PLIERS**
- **ROUND-NOSE PLIERS**
- **WIRE CUTTERS**
- **SUPER GLUE OR JEWELRY GLUE**

application

1. Take the 10 tan resistors and cut one lead completely off each one. Trim the remaining lead to about ½ inch (1.3 cm). Use round-nose pliers to loop all the ends.

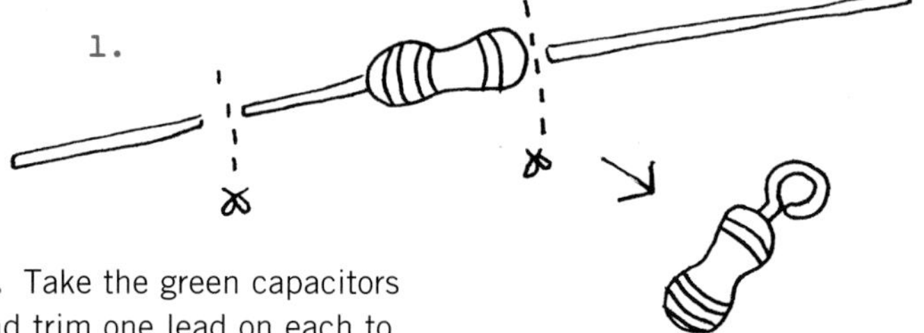

2. Take the green capacitors and trim one lead on each to ½ inch (1.3 cm). Trim the other lead a tiny bit longer than ½ inch.

3. Loop both ends of each capacitor.

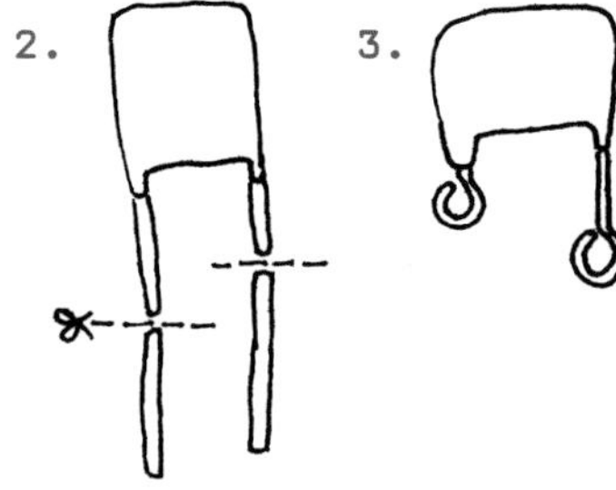

4. Attach two resistors to the short lead on each capacitor, and three to the longer lead.

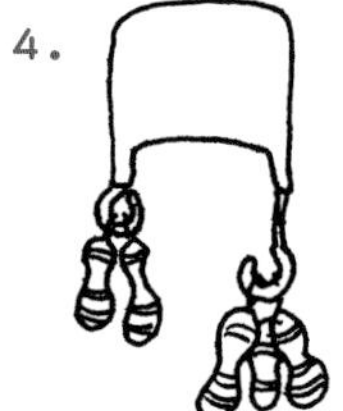

5. Put a dot of glue on the back of each capacitor and press on an earring base. Let dry.

5.

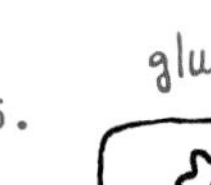

glue on earring base

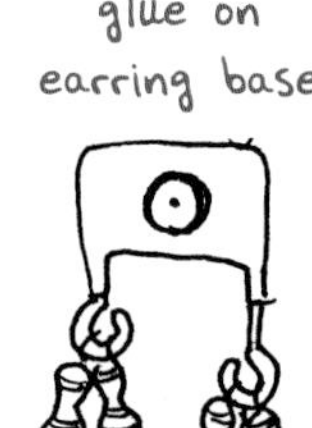

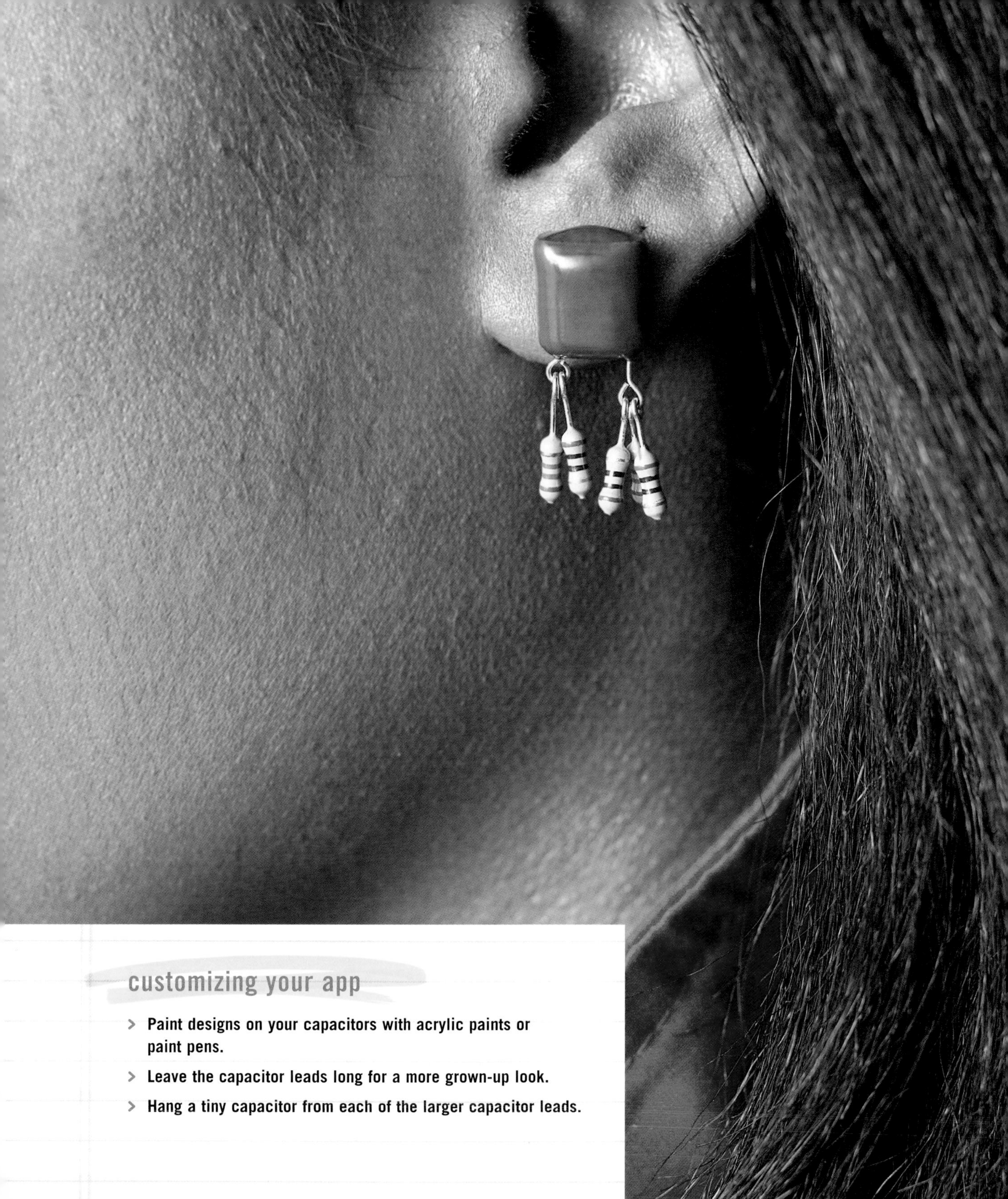

customizing your app

- Paint designs on your capacitors with acrylic paints or paint pens.
- Leave the capacitor leads long for a more grown-up look.
- Hang a tiny capacitor from each of the larger capacitor leads.

{easy}

Orange You Happy Dangles

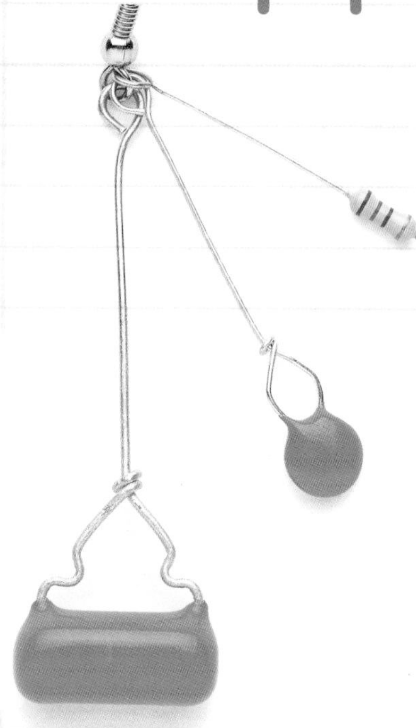

Who doesn't love a good—or even a bad—joke? I know I do. That's why I like to start my day by reading webcomics each morning. My favorites include *Dinosaur Comics*, *Diesel Sweeties*, and *Achewood*. I named these earrings in honor of all things funny, whether they be webcomics or your best friend.

application

1. Begin by performing the capacitor wrap on all of the orange capacitors (see page 26). Then loop all the ends with your round-nose pliers.

2. Cut one lead completely off each of the tan resistors and loop the remaining lead with round-nose pliers.

3. Attach all pieces to the French earwire, then repeat for the other earring.

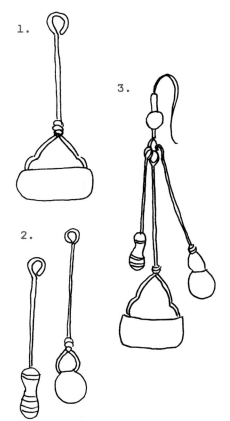

COMPONENTS AND HARDWARE

- 2 BRIGHT ORANGE CAPACITORS {Allied part number: 862-0214}
- 2 DULL ORANGE CAPACITORS {Allied part number: 507-0774}
- 2 SMALL TAN RESISTORS {Radio Shack part number: 271-308}
- 2 FRENCH EARWIRES
- NEEDLE-NOSE PLIERS
- ROUND-NOSE PLIERS
- WIRE CLIPPERS

customizing your app

- Make your earring into a pendant by adding a jump ring instead of an earwire and hanging it from a chain or cord.
- Use a small chain of resistors instead of one long one.
- Use waterproof permanent markers or glitter pens to draw a design on the large capacitor.

{medium}

Computer Confetti Dangles

I love to wear lots of different colors, and these earrings let me do exactly that! LEDs come in almost every color of the rainbow, so you can really get creative with your color schemes and patterns in these darling dangles.

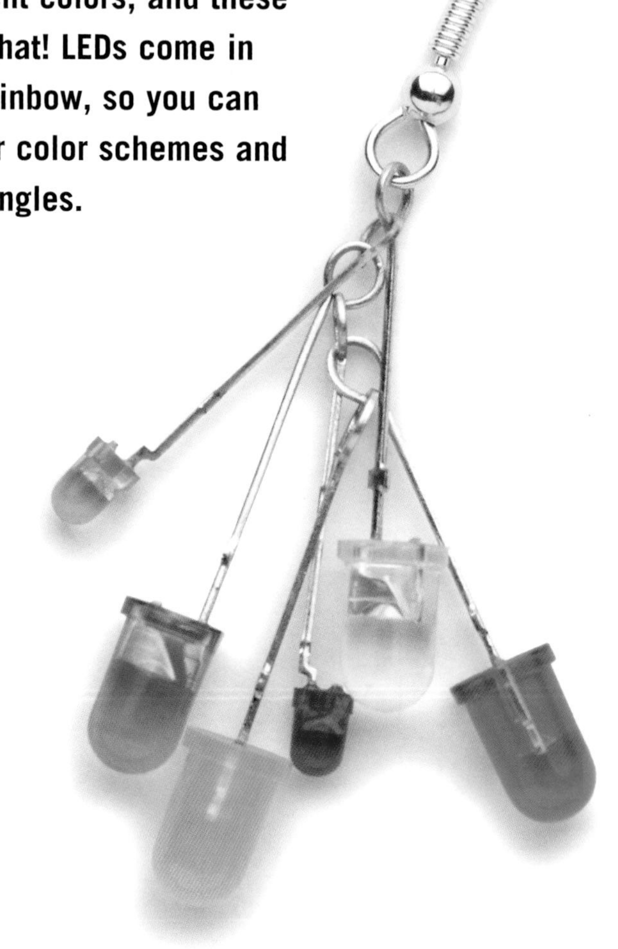

COMPONENTS AND HARDWARE

- 2 SMALL RED LEDS {Allied part number: 431-0239}
- 2 YELLOW LEDS {Allied part number: 431-0208}
- 2 GREEN LEDS {Allied part number: 431-0170}
- 2 SMALL LIGHT BLUE LEDS {Allied part number: 431-0220}
- 2 CLEAR LEDS {Allied part number: 431-0155}
- 2 PURPLE LEDS {Allied part number: 980-0094}
- 2 FRENCH EARWIRES
- NEEDLE-NOSE PLIERS
- ROUND-NOSE PLIERS
- WIRE CLIPPERS

more

application

1. Take all of your LEDs and cut one lead completely off each one. Then loop the ends of the remaining leads.

2. Take one LED in each color and string them together by their loops for a cascade effect (see illustration). Try to avoid hanging two LEDs from the same color or your LEDs will get bunched up. Repeat for the other earring, and remember to string both in the same order!

3. Attach each bundle of LEDs to an earwire by the top loop.

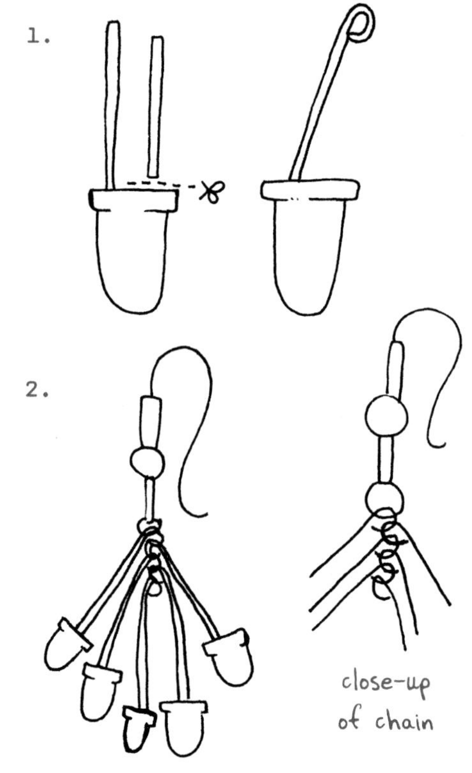

customizing your app

- **Mix resistors and LEDs on the same bunch for a more varied look.**
- **Make a super long pendant out of a bunch of LEDs.**
- **Use only one color of LEDs for a more subdued or uniform palette.**

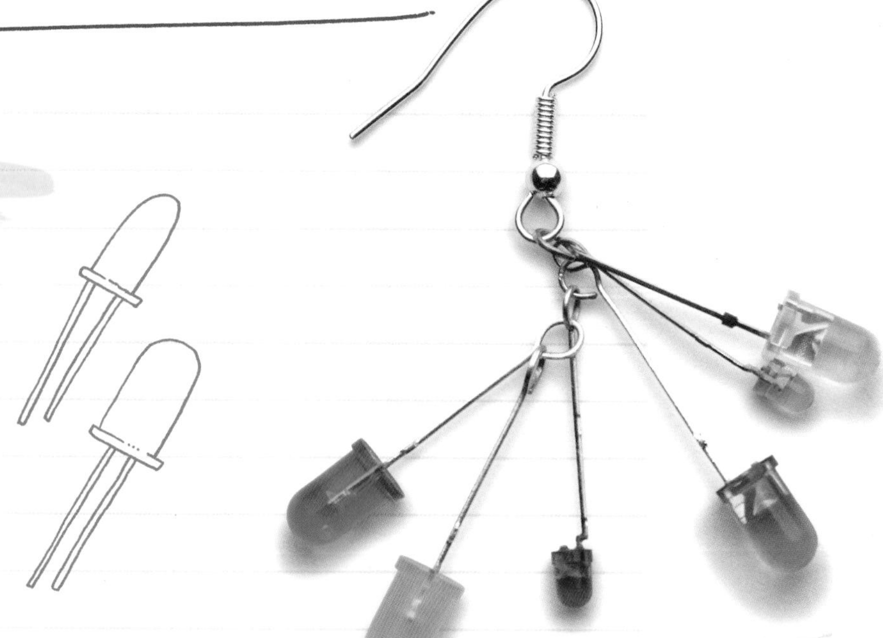

TOP 10 LIST FEMALE GEEK ICONS

1 **ADA BYRON KING, COUNTESS OF LOVELACE:** created the very first computer "program," way back in the 1880s!

2 **GRACE MURRAY HOPPER:** United States naval officer who invented the first computer code compiler

3 **HEDY LAMARR:** famous actress who also helped create frequency hopping, which is used today in cordless telephones and WiFi Internet

4 **ROBERTA WILLIAMS:** pioneered work in video adventure games with graphics

5 **KARI BYRON:** cast member of Discovery Channel's hit series *MythBusters*

6 **TINA FEY:** comedy television writer, actress, and all-around geek leading lady

7 **CYNTHIA BREAZEAL:** associate professor at MIT and leading humanoid robot researcher

8 **CATERINA FAKE:** cofounder of Flickr.com

9 **REBECCA BLOOD:** author of *The Weblog Handbook*

10 **LISA SIMPSON:** cartoon character geek

These bright Computer Confetti Dangles are a colorful complement to my Tina Fey-style nerd-girl glasses.

COMPUTER CONFETTI

{medium}

Lightning Dangles

One of my favorite color combinations is blue and yellow, and that's what inspired me to put together this simple pair of dangles. Not only will you look cool wearing these, but the mini lightbulbs will inspire great ideas all day!

COMPONENTS AND HARDWARE

- 2 BROWN RESISTORS {Allied part number: 895-0937}
- 2 YELLOW LEDS {Allied part number: 431-0144}
- 2 BLUE CAPACITORS {Allied part number: 266-0209}
- 2 CLEAR LIGHTBULBS {Allied part number: 749-1386}
- 2 FRENCH EARWIRES
- NEEDLE-NOSE PLIERS
- ROUND-NOSE PLIERS
- WIRE CLIPPERS

application

1. Begin by trimming all the brown resistor leads to about ½ inch (1.3 cm). Then take your blue capacitors and perform the capacitor wrap on each (see page 26).

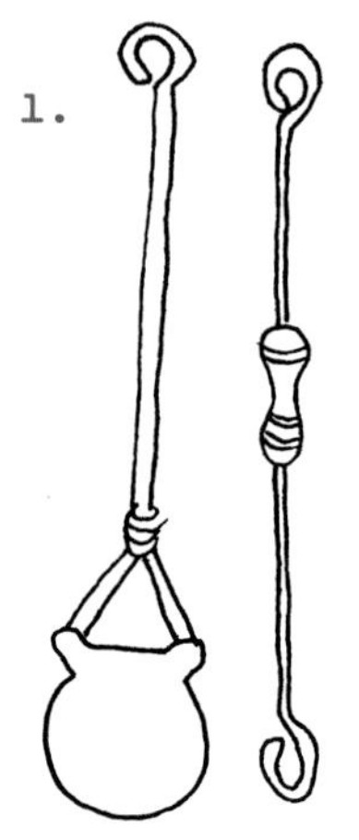

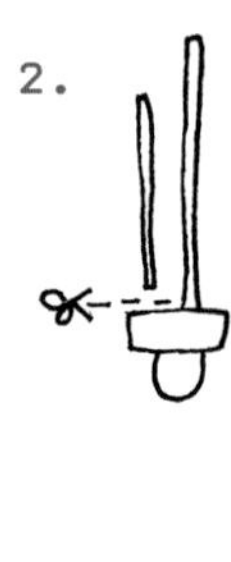

2. Take your yellow LEDs and cut one lead completely off each one. Take the yellow LEDs, blue capacitors, and brown resistors and loop all the leads with your round-nose pliers.

3. Take your lightbulb and pinch the very ends of the thin leads with your needle-nose pliers. Hold the bulb in your hand and twist it with your fingers until the leads are tightly entwined. Use your round-nose pliers to loop the ends.

4. Hang your brown capacitor and the lightbulb from the earwire loop, then take the yellow LED and the blue capacitor and hang them from the lower loop of the brown resistor. Repeat for the second earring.

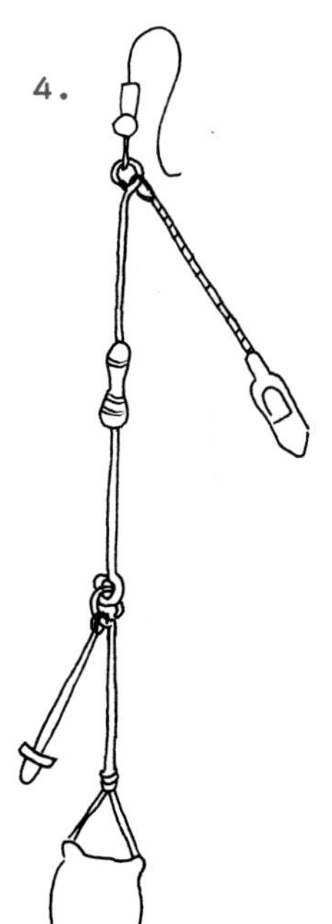

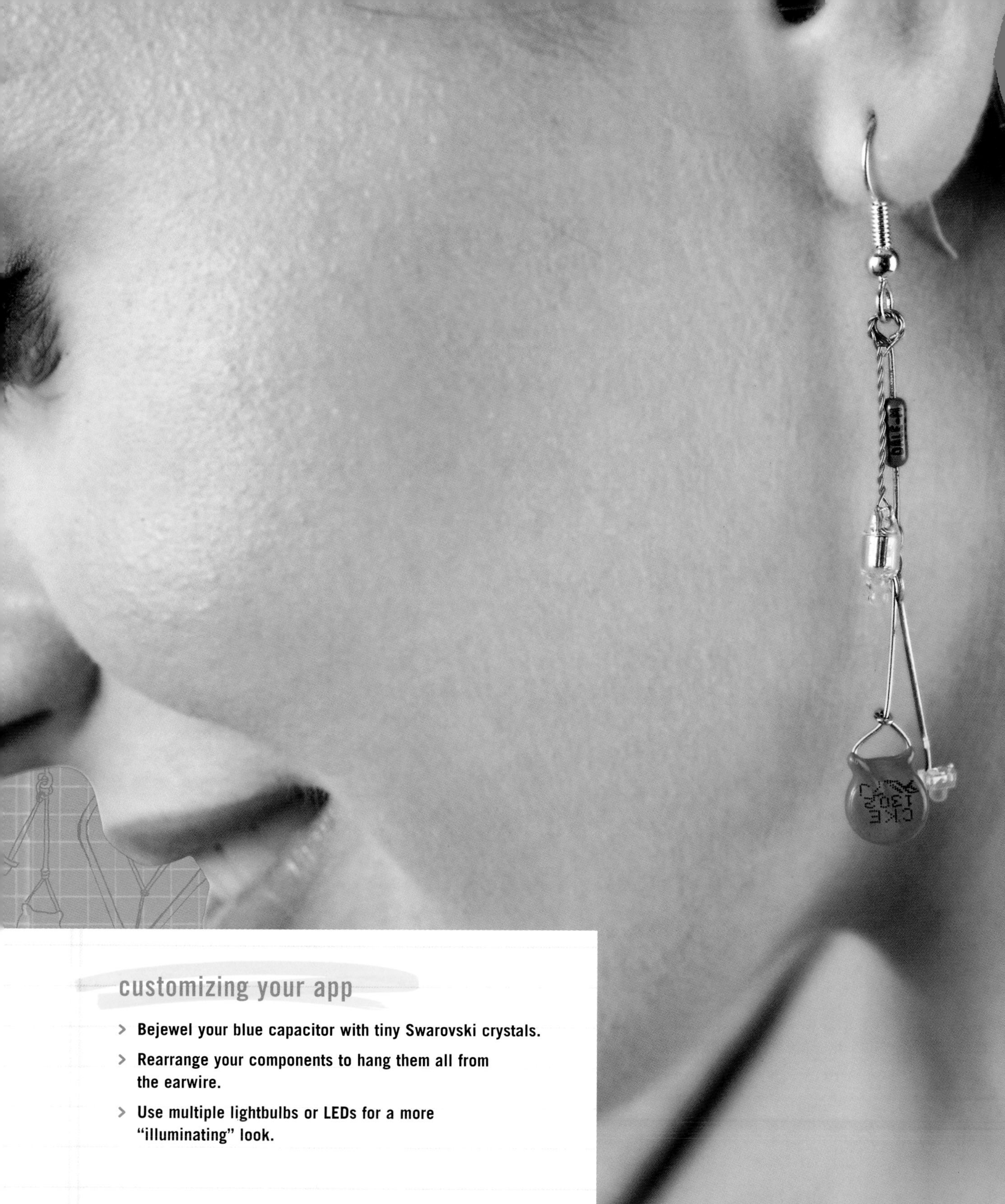

customizing your app

- Bejewel your blue capacitor with tiny Swarovski crystals.
- Rearrange your components to hang them all from the earwire.
- Use multiple lightbulbs or LEDs for a more "illuminating" look.

{medium}

Radial Raindrops

This past year we had a ridiculous amount of rain, which is a nightmare when you're always walking across campus to your next class. It tends to make people a little grouchy. So I made these earrings to cheer myself up on rainy days—and to look great, too!

application

1. Take the tan resistors and trim both leads on each one to a little less than ½ inch (1.3 cm).

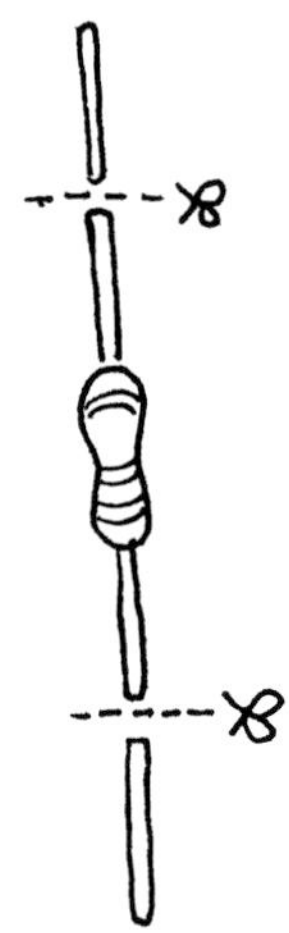

2. Use round-nose pliers to loop one lead on each resistor. Loop the end of the other lead perpendicular to the rounded end on the opposite side. In other words, your loops should face in different directions.

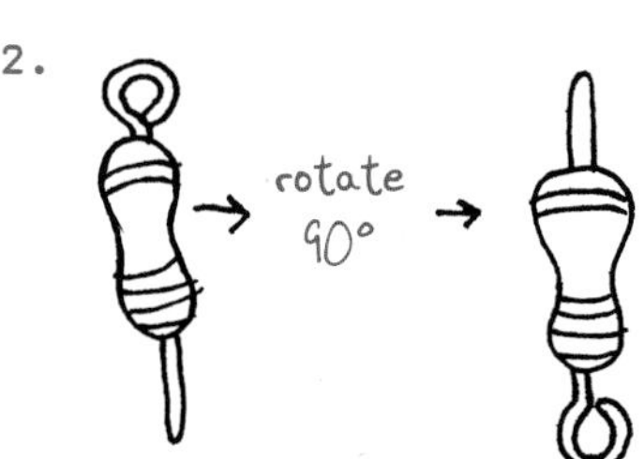

COMPONENTS AND HARDWARE

- 4 MEDIUM TAN RESISTORS {Radio Shack part number: 271-1106}
- 2 MEDIUM BLUE CAPACITORS {Radio Shack part number: 272-1053}
- 2 FRENCH EARWIRES
- 2 LARGE TEARDROP HOOPS
- NEEDLE-NOSE PLIERS
- ROUND-NOSE PLIERS
- WIRE CLIPPERS

more

3. Chain two resistors together (see page 25). Attach one end of the chain to a teardrop hoop and the other end to an earwire. Repeat for the other earring.

4. Do the capacitor wrap on both blue capacitors (see page 26).

5. Twist the loop at the top perpendicular to the capacitor. Attach it to the inside loop of the teardrop hoop. This part is a little tricky, so try using the very tips of the needle-nose pliers to close the gap. Repeat for the other earring.

Radial Raindrops

customizing your app

- Add or subtract the number of resistors attached to the chain in step 2.
- Attach a bunch of resistors to the center of your raindrop hoops.
- Use one uncut resistor instead of two trimmed ones.

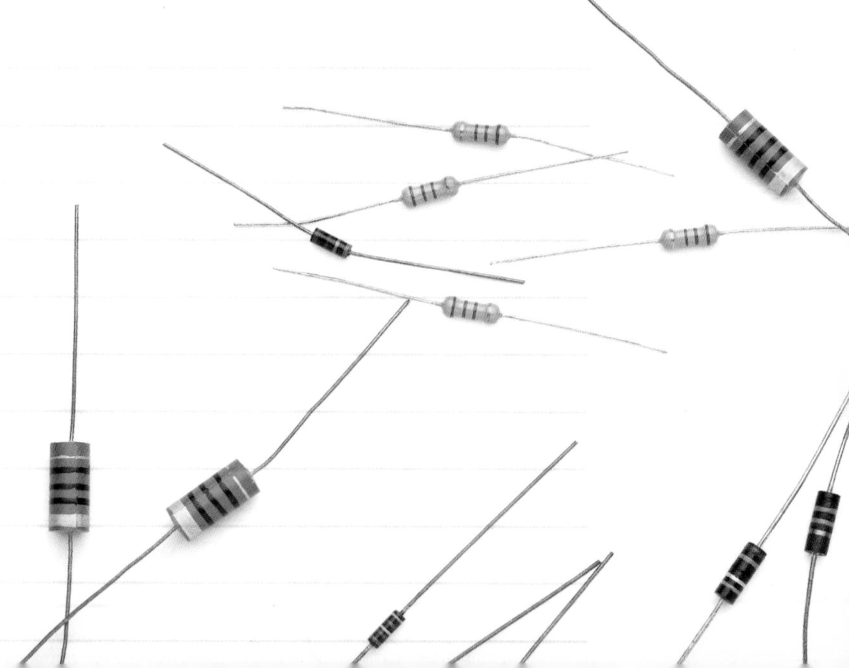

Shanaé's cropped cut shows off her Radial Raindrops perfectly—long earrings and short hair are a super cute combination.

RADIAL RAINDROPS

RANDOM TECHIE TRIVIA

HERBERT HOOVER's face was the first thing seen on television screens when they were unveiled. The sound was carried over telephone wires.

The word "**ROBOT**" was coined in 1920 by Czech writer Karel Capek, for his play *R.U.R. (Rossum's Universal Robots)*.

HEWLETT-PACKARD was formed in a garage in Palo Alto, California, during the Great Depression.

ATARI attempted to enter the personal computer market in 1979, but their computers were taken off the market because the public didn't take their product seriously.

GRACE MURRAY HOPPER popularized the term computer "bug" after discovering a moth stuck in a computer relay at Harvard University.

The first mass-produced computer was the IBM 650, which debuted in the early 1950s.

ASTEROIDS was the first video game to allow high-scoring players to enter their three initials to be stored with their high score.

SPACE INVADERS was the first arcade game to save users' high scores in the system.

In 1983, **NINTENDO** initially offered to Atari distribution rights to the Nintendo Entertainment System (NES). Negotiations fell through, and Nintendo brought the NES to the States in 1985.

{medium}

Chandelier Circuits

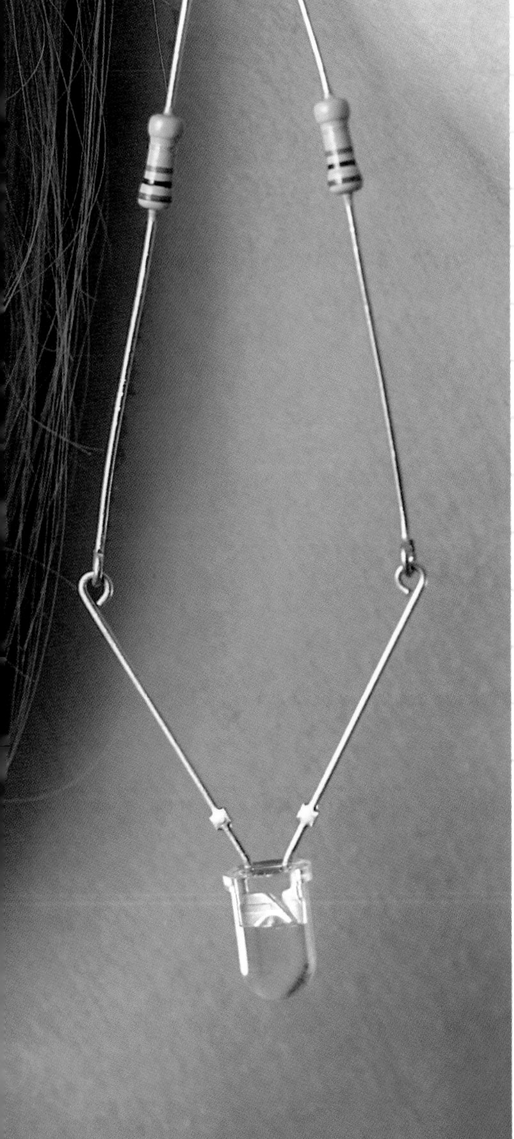

You've landed a date with Mr. Dreamy, and you need that little extra-alluring *something* to accentuate your look. These earrings are sure to attract attention on any rendezvous.

COMPONENTS AND HARDWARE

- 2 CLEAR LEDS {Allied part number: 431-0167}
- 4 SKY BLUE RESISTORS {Allied part number: 648-0204}
- 2 FRENCH EARWIRES
- NEEDLE-NOSE PLIERS
- ROUND-NOSE PLIERS
- WIRE CUTTERS

application

1. Trim the leads on both clear LEDs to equal lengths (one lead is usually longer than the other).

1.

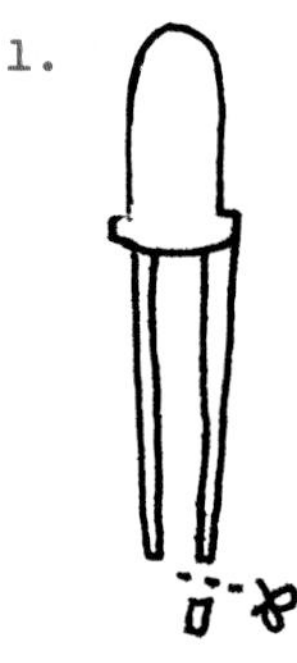

more

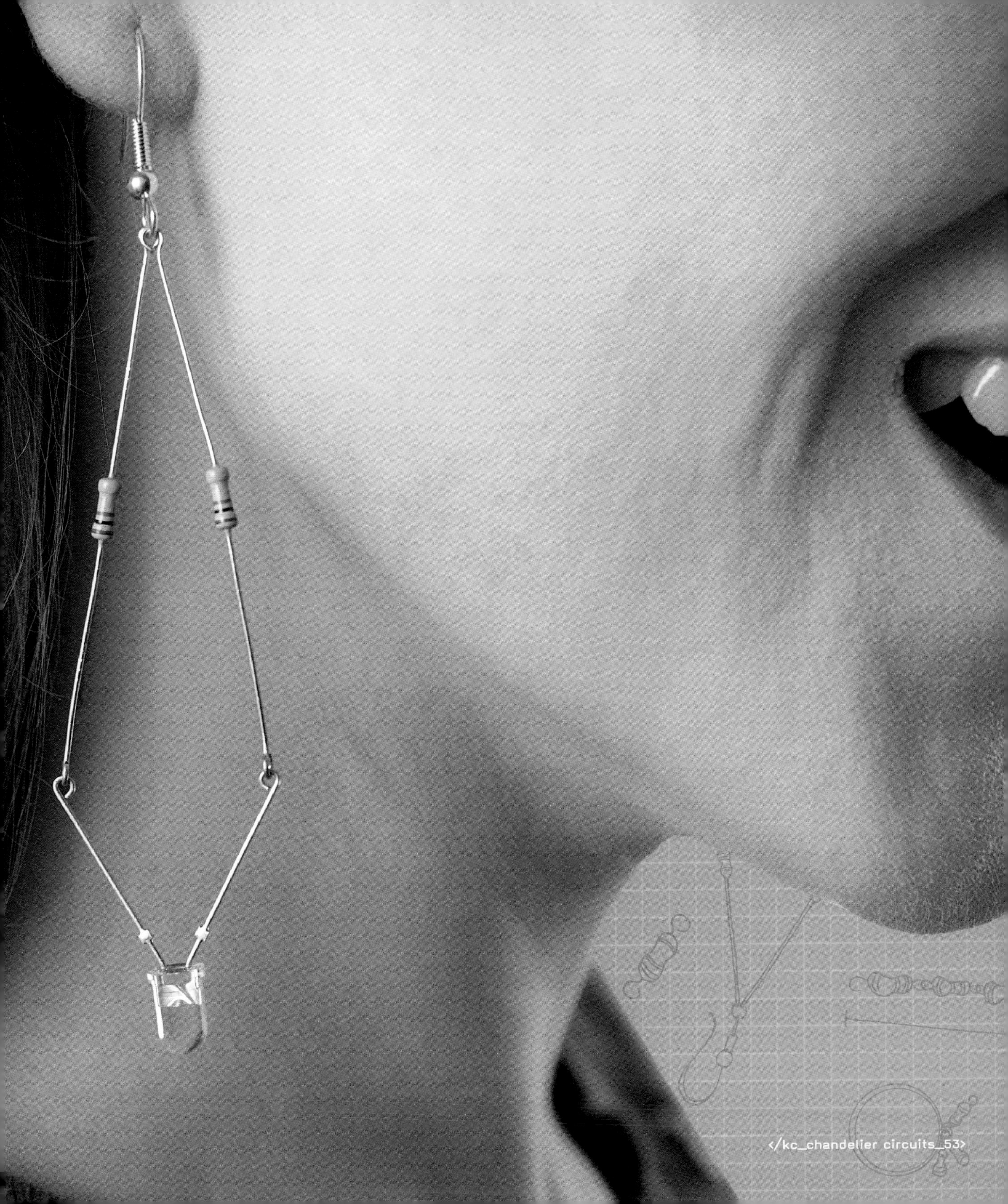

2. Hold the LED and spread the leads into a V shape. The wider the V, the shorter the earrings. (Try not to manipulate the ends too much or they will break off!) Use round-nose pliers to loop the end of each lead toward the center.

3. Take the sky blue resistors and use round-nose pliers to loop one lead on each. Loop the end of the other lead perpendicular to the first. It is important that the lead ends are in this configuration so they will connect the LED to the earwire correctly and not kink.

4. Attach one resistor to each lead on the LED. Carefully connect the other end of each resistor to an earwire. Repeat for the other earring. It might take a little practice to get the arrangement right so it hangs nicely, but don't give up!

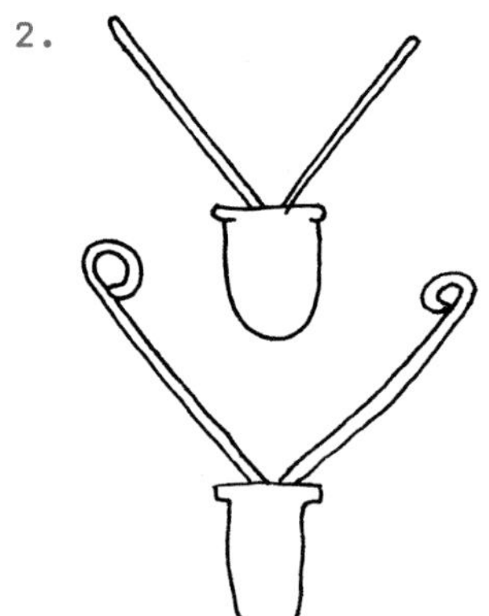

CHANDELIER CIRCUITS

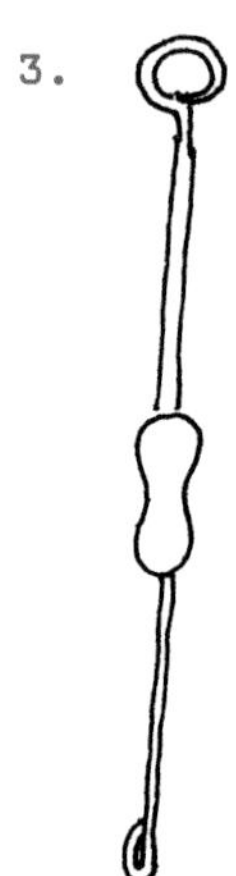

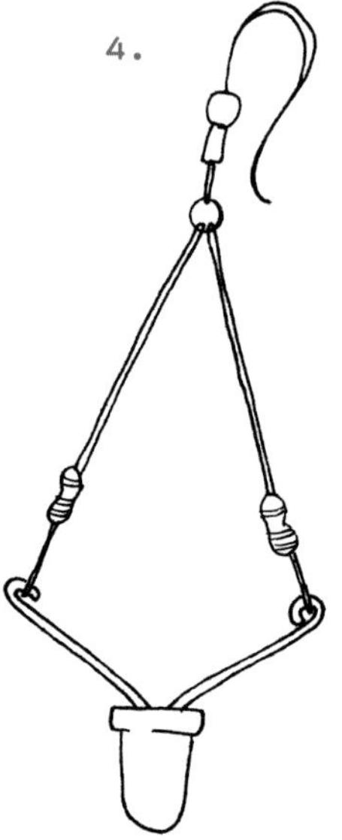

customizing your app

- **Use a chain of trimmed resistors to connect the LED to the earwire.**
- **Use a long piece of colorful jewelry wire instead of resistors.**
- **String beads onto all of the leads.**

TOP 10 LISTS

MUST-HAVE GEEK ELECTRONICS

1 **iPhone**
2 **Laptop computer**
3 **Wireless router**
4 **TI-89 calculator**
5 **Casio wristwatch**
6 **Desktop computer**
7 **External hard drive**
8 **Nintendo Wii**
9 **TiVo**
10 **GPS (Global Positioning System)**

SOCIAL NETWORKING WEBSITES

1 **Facebook**
2 **YouTube**
3 **Flickr**
4 **Twitter**
5 **del.icio.us**
6 **Last.fm**
7 **Digg**
8 **MySpace**
9 **Reddit**
10 **Mint**

{medium}

Byte Bouquets

A virtual bouquet of components for your ears! These earrings are a great way to use up excess capacitors and resistors, and also to play with different color combinations and component lengths.

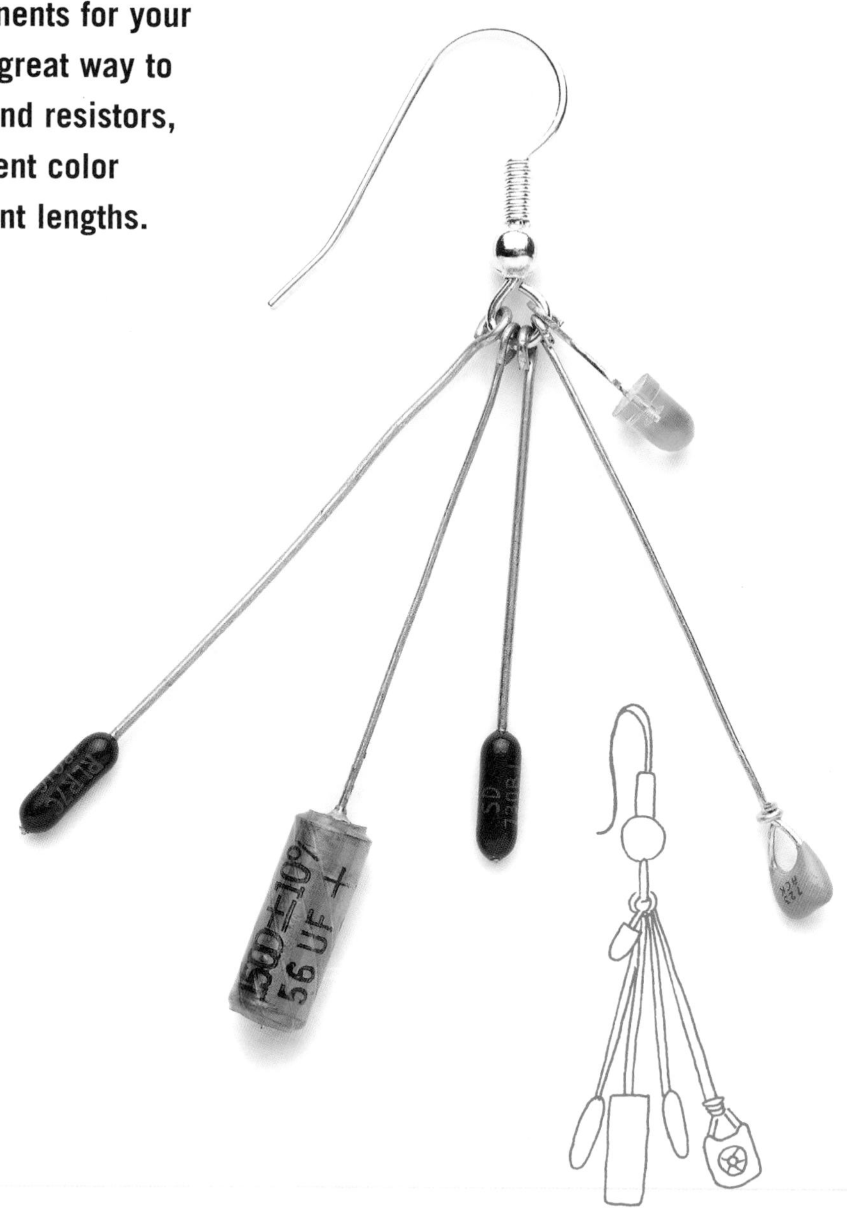

COMPONENTS AND HARDWARE

- 2 CYAN CAPACITORS {Allied part number: 929-1529}
- 2 TINY YELLOW CAPACITORS {Allied part number: 881-0417}
- 4 NAVY RESISTORS {Allied part number: 895-3154}
- 2 TINY BLUE LEDS {Allied part number: 431-0219}
- 2 FRENCH EARWIRES
- 2 5SS XILION SWAROVSKI CRYSTALS
- NEEDLE-NOSE PLIERS
- ROUND-NOSE PLIERS
- WIRE CUTTERS
- SUPER GLUE OR JEWELRY GLUE

more

application

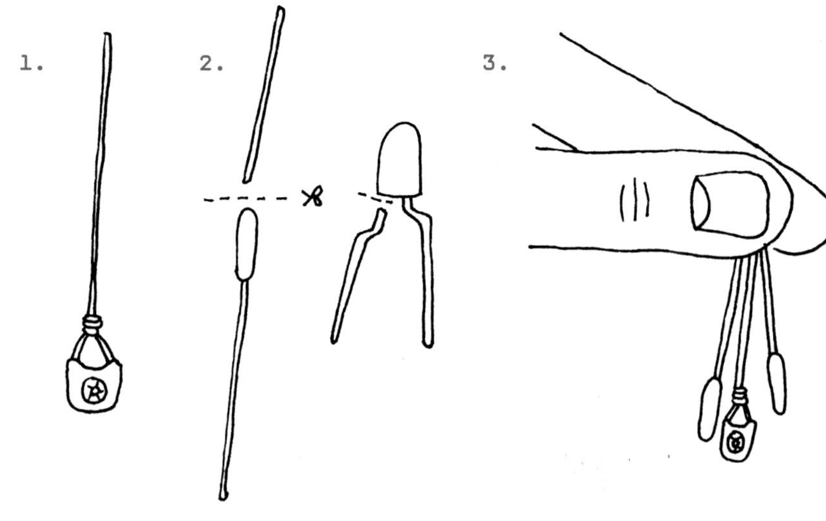

1. Take the yellow capacitors and do a capacitor wrap on each (see page 26). Put a tiny dot of glue on both and attach a Swarovski crystal. Let dry.

2. Cut one lead completely off each of the navy resistors and the blue LED.

3. Gather all of the pieces—including your now-sparkly yellow capacitors—and play around with the arrangement for each "bouquet," deciding how long each should be. I tend to find a centerpiece and arrange the rest of the components around it.

4. Trim the lead on each piece to accommodate your chosen arrangement. Then use round-nose pliers to loop the ends.

5. Hang all the pieces from an earwire. Repeat for the other earring.

customizing your app

- **Change the color scheme with alternative parts.**
- **Add more bling to your components with many more crystals.**
- **Use only capacitors or resistors in your arrangement.**

Use this same technique with different components and colors to create an infinite variety of styles.

GEEK TRIVIA Q&A

1 > Which famous inventor was physically revolted by jewelry, notably pearl earrings?

2 > This component is made from a variety of materials, such as carbon or metal film; it reduces the flow of an electric current.

3 > In 1963, Douglas Engelbart invented this popular computer device.

4 > What does AC/DC—a commonly used acronym in the electrical industry—stand for?

5 > How much gold does the jewelry industry use per year?

6 > Where does the word "jewelry" originate?

7 > These were used by English traders as currency.

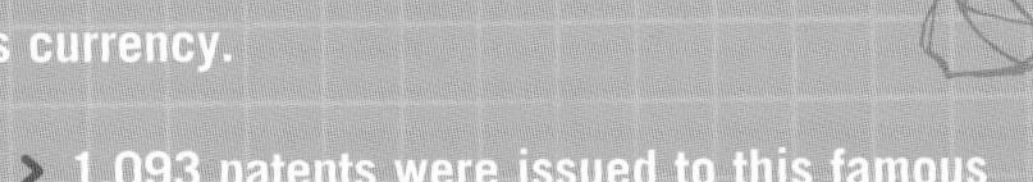

8 > 1,093 patents were issued to this famous inventor—more than any other person in U.S. history.

9 > These are often used as small indicator lights on electronic devices.

10 > When Superman made his debut in Action Comics in 1938, he didn't live in Metropolis. Where were his first stomping grounds?

11 > What famous medal depicts three naked men with their hands on one another's shoulders?

12 > Which product was the first to have a bar code on its packaging?

13 > What was the cost of the very first Apple I computer sold in 1976?

14 > What do many consider their all-time favorite geek movie?

15 > This Harvard freshman dropped out of college so he could devote his time to writing computer programs.

16 > What does USB stand for?

17 > Who introduced the metal platinum into jewelry making?

18 > These are often used in electric and electronic circuits as energy storage devices.

19 > What is the world's leading professional association for the advancement of technology?

20 > This is a group of computers and associated devices that share a common communications line or wireless link.

1 > Nikola Tesla **2 >** Resistor **3 >** Computer mouse **4 >** Alternating Current/Direct Current **5 >** Approximately 1,000 tons **6 >** It is an old French word meaning "joy" or "gladness." **7 >** Beads **8 >** Thomas Edison **9 >** LEDs (light-emitting diodes) **10 >** New York City **11 >** The Nobel Peace Prize **12 >** Wrigley's gum **13 >** $600 **14 >** *2001: A Space Odyssey* **15 >** Bill Gates **16 >** Universal Serial Bus **17 >** Cartier **18 >** Capacitors **19 >** IEEE, or Institute of Electrical and Electronics Engineers, Inc. **20 >** LAN, or Local Area Network

{hard}

Broadband Hoops

Capacitors are components that store energy in whatever circuit they are soldered into—and these sparkly, loopy earrings definitely store fun, whether for a night out on the town or a quiet afternoon reading. Don't let anyone know your secret!

COMPONENTS AND HARDWARE

- 2 MEDIUM BROWN CAPACITORS {Allied part number: 613-0546}
- 4 4MM SWAROVSKI CRYSTAL BEADS
- 50 10SS XILION SWAROVSKI FLAT-BACK CRYSTALS
- NEEDLE-NOSE PLIERS
- ROUND-NOSE PLIERS
- WIRE CUTTERS
- SUPER GLUE OR JEWELRY GLUE
- TWEEZERS

FOR QUICK VERSION:

- PLAIN HOOP EARRINGS

FOR SLOWER VERSION:

- 2 FRENCH EARWIRES
- 9–10 INCHES 41-GAUGE JEWELRY WIRE

application

1. If you're using preformed hoop earrings, skip to step 5. If you're using jewelry wire to make hoops, start by finding a mold around which to make the perfect circle. I used a film canister, but you can use any circular object that has a diameter of about 1½ inches (3.8 cm).

2. Cut your piece of jewelry wire in half. Take one piece and use round-nose pliers to bend 1 inch (2.5 cm) of one end into a 90-degree angle.

3. Place the angled end at the top of your mold; this will become the "tail." Then gently wrap the rest of the wire around the mold.

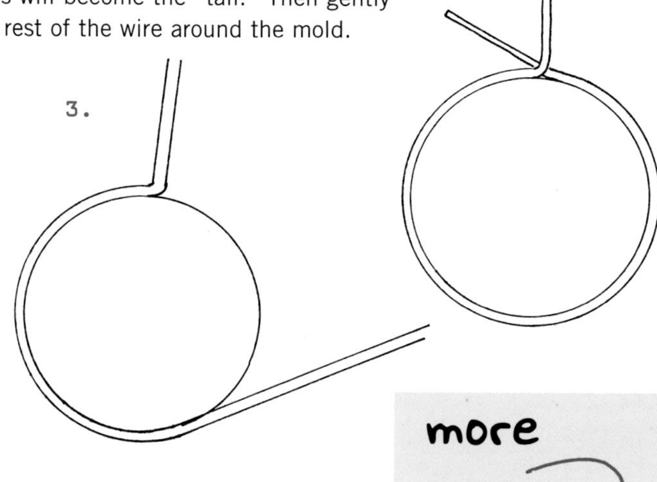

more

4. Wrap the remaining wire around the tail at the top and make a loop (just as in the capacitor wrap on page 26). Trim off any excess wire.

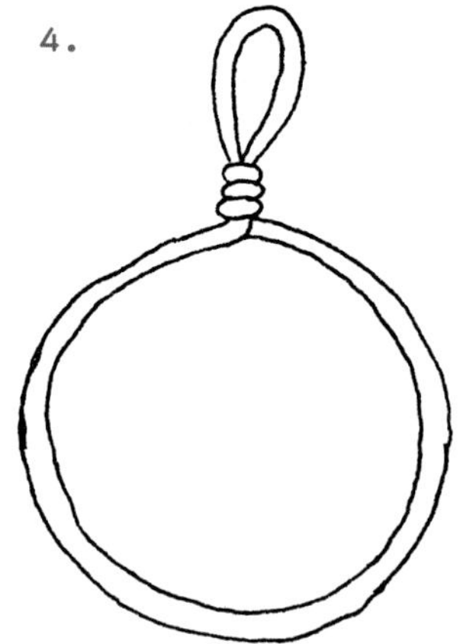

5. Slide an earwire onto the loop to complete the hoop.

6. Repeat steps 2 to 3 to make a second hoop with the other piece of wire.

7. Take a brown capacitor and slide two Swarovski crystal beads onto one lead. Do the capacitor wrap, using the lead holding the beads to wrap around the other lead. Clip off the excess lead and trim the remaining lead to about ½ inch (1.3 cm). Use round-nose pliers to loop the end perpendicular to the capacitor. Repeat with the other capacitor.

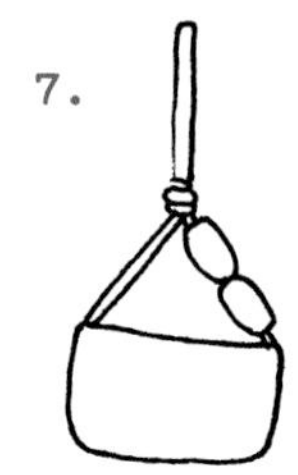

8. This is where it gets a little . . . er . . . sticky. Lay the capacitors on a flat surface in a well-ventilated space. Dab three dots of glue on one capacitor and, using tweezers, gently place crystals on the glue. Complete three more rows of three crystals each. Let dry, then decorate the reverse side. Repeat for the other capacitor.

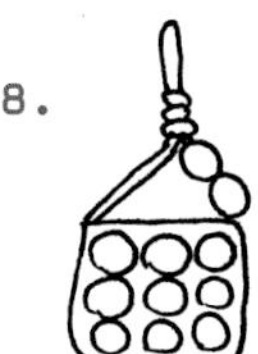

9. When the capacitors are completely dry, use your needle-nose pliers to attach them to the hoops.

customizing your app

- **Make a coordinating bangle bracelet (see page 66).**
- **Wrap your hoop around a different mold shape, or try squares or ovals.**
- **String several charms onto each hoop, or change the charm every day.**
- **Use different colors of Swarovski crystals.**

TOP 10 LIST GEEKY DATE NIGHTS

1. Catch a midnight viewing of *Star Wars* at an independent film house
2. Stake out your favorite writers and gamers at ComicCon
3. Find a Trivia Night at a local cafe and win prizes testing all your useless info
4. Get your video gaming on at home with Mario, Link, and Sonic
5. Check out the night sky and see who can name the most constellations
6. Host a board game night with friends
7. Spend a few hours—and quarters—at the arcade playing old-school video games
8. Go hear the indie band lineup at your favorite club
9. Hunt for treasures with your GPS Geocaching game
10. One word: bowling

BROADBAND earrings

classic video games

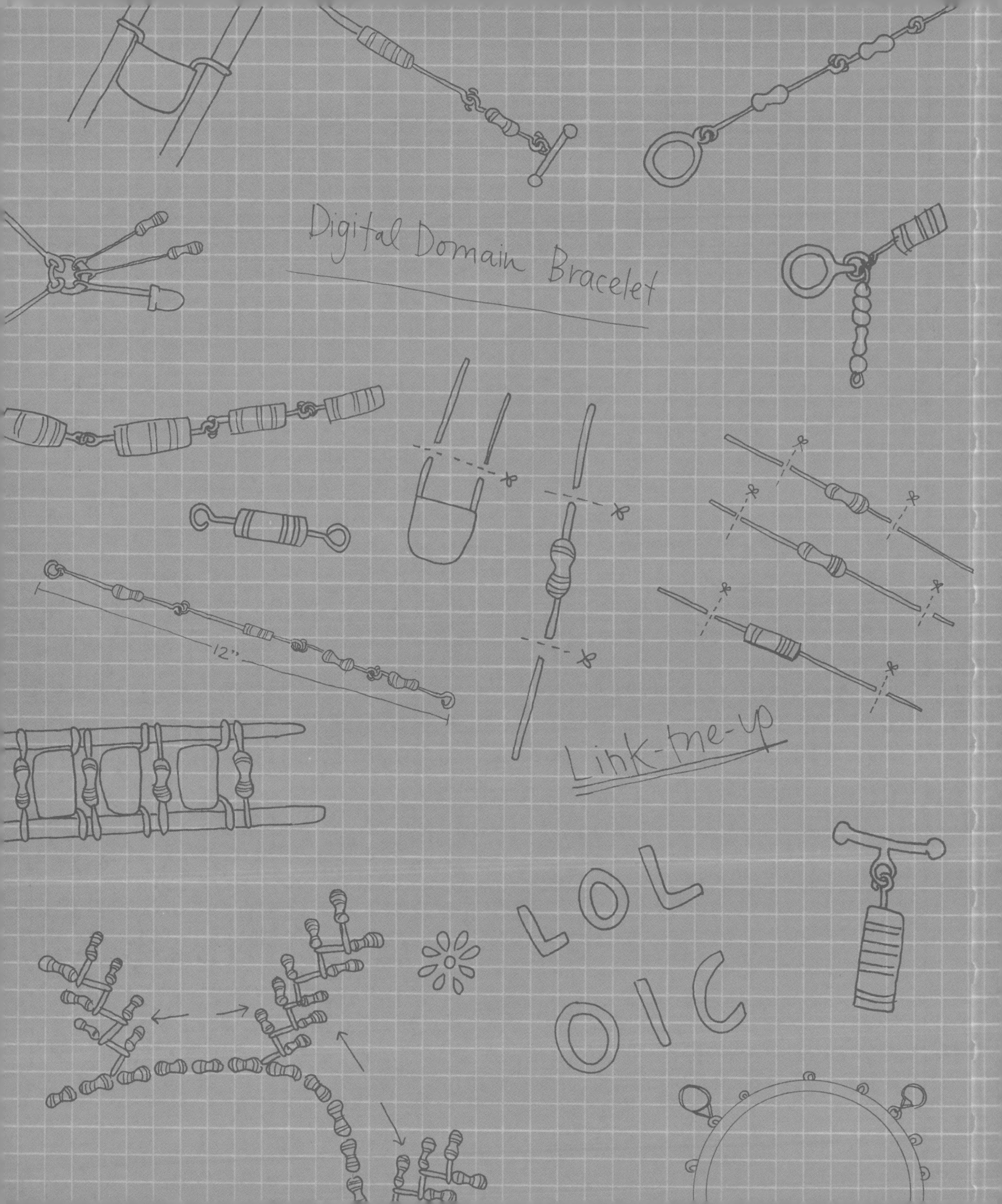

Digital Domain Bracelet
12"
Link-me-up
LOL
OIC

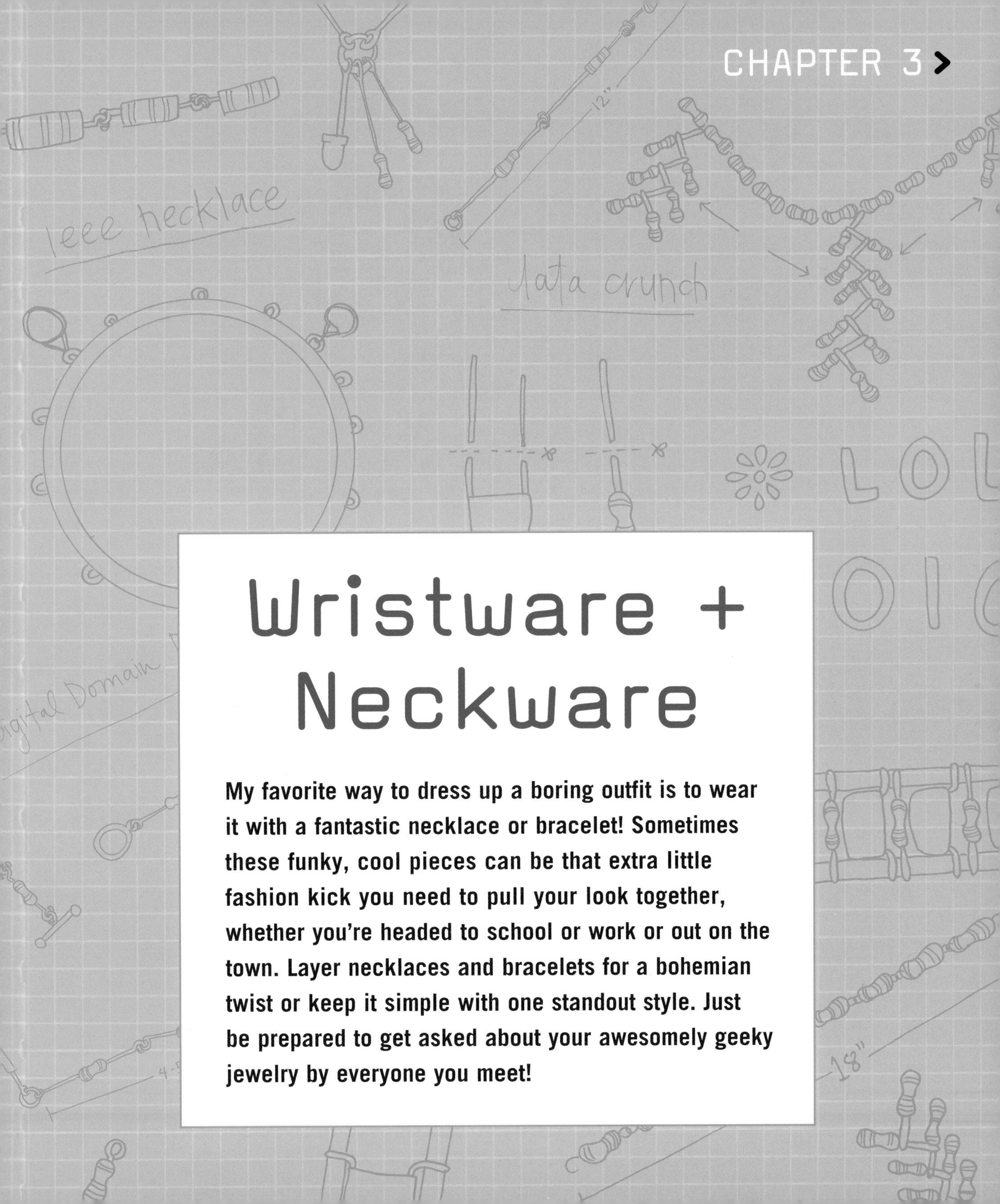

CHAPTER 3 >

Wristware + Neckware

My favorite way to dress up a boring outfit is to wear it with a fantastic necklace or bracelet! Sometimes these funky, cool pieces can be that extra little fashion kick you need to pull your look together, whether you're headed to school or work or out on the town. Layer necklaces and bracelets for a bohemian twist or keep it simple with one standout style. Just be prepared to get asked about your awesomely geeky jewelry by everyone you meet!

{easy}

Data Crunch Bracelet

The jingling sound made by the resistors on this bracelet reminds me of the sound computers make when they're "thinking." Everyone has heard it and has gotten frustrated waiting for it to finish. One thing's for sure: You won't get frustrated by anything about this bracelet!

application

1. Do the capacitor wrap on each of the cyan capacitors (see page 26).

2. Attach the loop on each capacitor to a loop on the bracelet, spacing the three capacitors evenly.

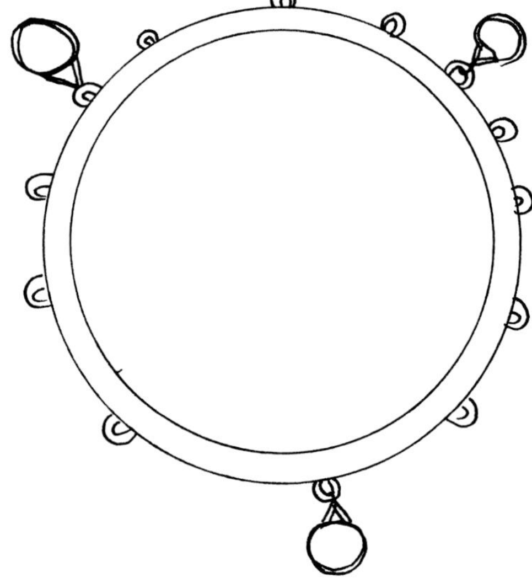

2.

COMPONENTS AND HARDWARE

- 3 SMALL CYAN CAPACITORS {Allied part number: 266-0107}
- 3 MEDIUM TAN RESISTORS {Radio Shack part number: 271-1122}
- 26 SMALL TAN RESISTORS {Radio Shack part number: 271-308}
- 1 BANGLE BRACELET WITH LOOPS
- ROUND-NOSE PLIERS
- NEEDLE-NOSE PLIERS
- WIRE CUTTERS

more

24"
converse
allstars
12"

3. Cut one lead completely off each tan resistor. Trim the other lead to about ½ inch (1.3 cm) and round it into a loop with your round-nose pliers, but don't close the loop completely. I find it easiest to trim all the leads first, then loop them. The repetitive motion soon becomes pure muscle memory!

3.

data crunch

4. Attach each of the three medium resistors to the same loops holding the capacitors.

5. Connect the small resistors to the remaining loops all around the bracelet, two per loop.

5.

customizing your app

- Use more capacitors, packing as many onto each loop as possible.
- Leave the resistor leads longer and slide a bead onto each before looping the ends.
- Hang only capacitors around the bracelet.

TOP 10 LIST

MALE GEEK DREAMBOATS

1 **GREGG GILLIS:** biomedical engineer turned deejay/mash-up artist

2 **KEVIN ROSE:** creator of Digg.com and cohost of the weekly Diggnation podcast

3 **JON STEWART:** satirist and host of *The Daily Show*

4 **IRA GLASS:** storyteller, moderator, and host of *This American Life*

5 **BRAD NEELY:** animator and creator of the comic series *Wizard People, Dear Readers*

6 **JASON SCHWARTZMAN:** actor who's in several Wes Anderson movies (swoon)

7 **BRUCE WAYNE:** I mean seriously, he's Batman.

8 **JOHN KRASINSKI:** actor who plays Jim on *The Office*

9 **DEMETRI MARTIN:** comedian, writer, and guest correspondent on *The Daily Show*

10 **MARIO:** Who can resist this video game hero?

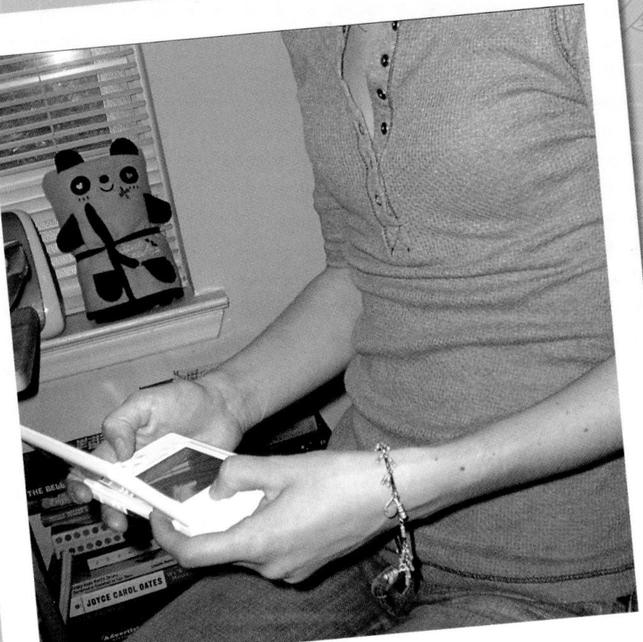

All eyes on the game! Unless you're wearing your Data Crunch bangle, which might be cause for distraction to any geeky guy waiting his turn....

{easy}

IEEE Necklace

IEEE stands for "Institute of Electrical and Electronics Engineers." These engineers spend all day using the materials that go into this necklace, so it seemed appropriate to tip my hat their way. Even though the end result looks like you spent hours putting everything together, this necklace is actually quite easy to make. And when you wear it, feel confident that you'll look absolutely electrifying.

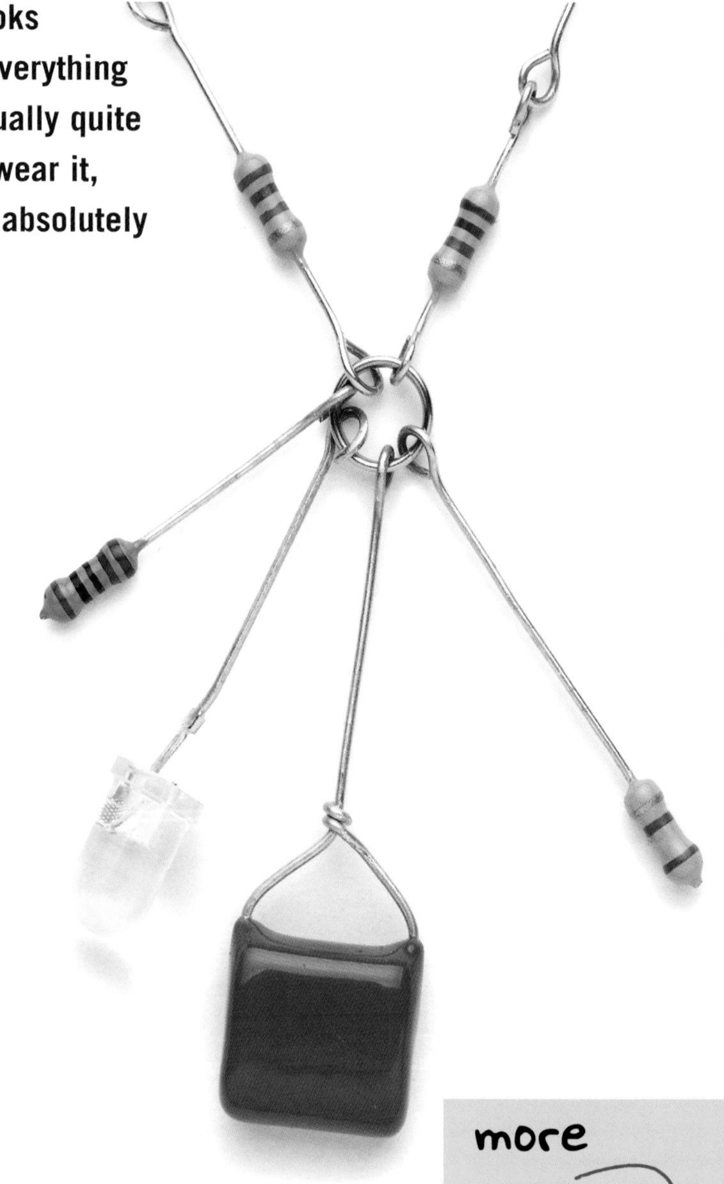

COMPONENTS AND HARDWARE

- 25 SMALL TAN RESISTORS {Radio Shack part number: 271-308}
- 5 SMALL BLUE RESISTORS {Radio Shack part number: 271-309}
- 3 MEDIUM TAN RESISTORS {Radio Shack part number: 271-306}
- 1 CLEAR LED {Allied part number: 431-0167}
- 1 SMALL CYAN CAPACITOR {Allied part number: 266-0107}
- 1 MEDIUM BROWN CAPACITOR {Allied part number: 613-0546}
- 1 TOGGLE CLASP
- 1 JUMP RING OR SPRING RING
- NEEDLE-NOSE PLIERS
- ROUND-NOSE PLIERS
- WIRE CUTTERS

more

application

1. Take one small tan resistor and one small blue resistor and set them aside for later.

2. Take the remaining resistors and trim the leads randomly to various lengths. When you're done, it might be helpful to organize them in two piles—one for resistors with longer leads, one for those with short leads.

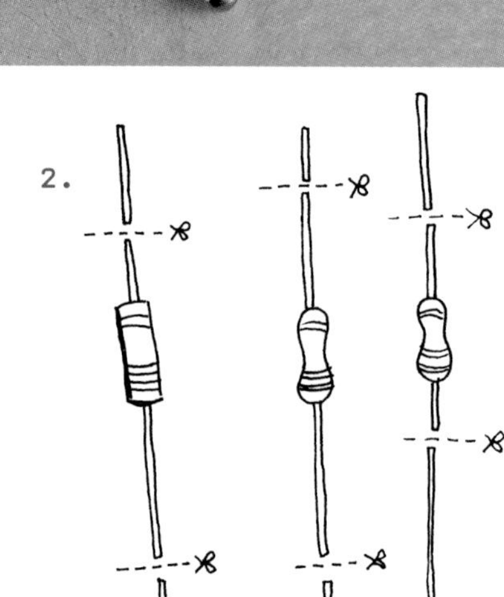

3. To start the chain, loop all the ends of the resistors. Then take the jump ring, attach a resistor, and start to build the chain of resistors until it's about 12 inches (30.5 cm) long. I like to put resistors with longer leads closest to the jump ring and those with super-short leads toward the clasp end.

4. Now attach a second chain to the same jump ring, also 12 inches (30.5 cm) long. Again, use resistors with longer leads closest to the jump ring and those with shorter leads toward the clasp end. You should end up with one 24-inch (61-cm) chain with the jump ring in the center.

5. Attach the toggle clasp components to the loops at both ends of the chain.

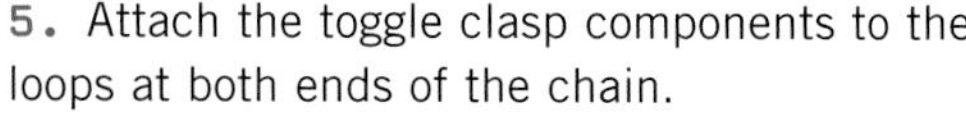

6. Take both capacitors and do the capacitor wrap on each (see page 26).

7. Attach the cyan capacitor about 4 to 5 inches (10 to 12 cm) from the jump ring on one side. Fasten the brown capacitor to the center jump ring.

8. Cut one lead completely off the clear LED and loop the other lead. Attach the lead to the jump ring.

9. Now take the two resistors you set aside in step 1. Cut one lead on each completely off and loop the end of the remaining lead. Attach both leads to the jump ring.

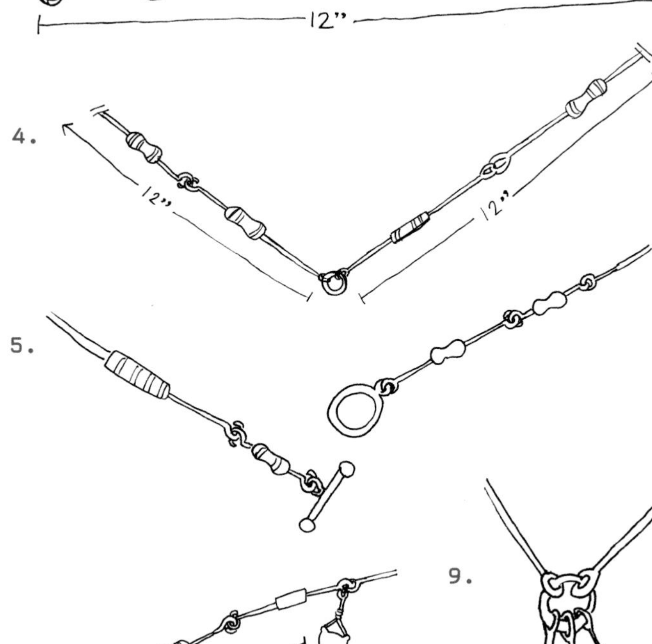

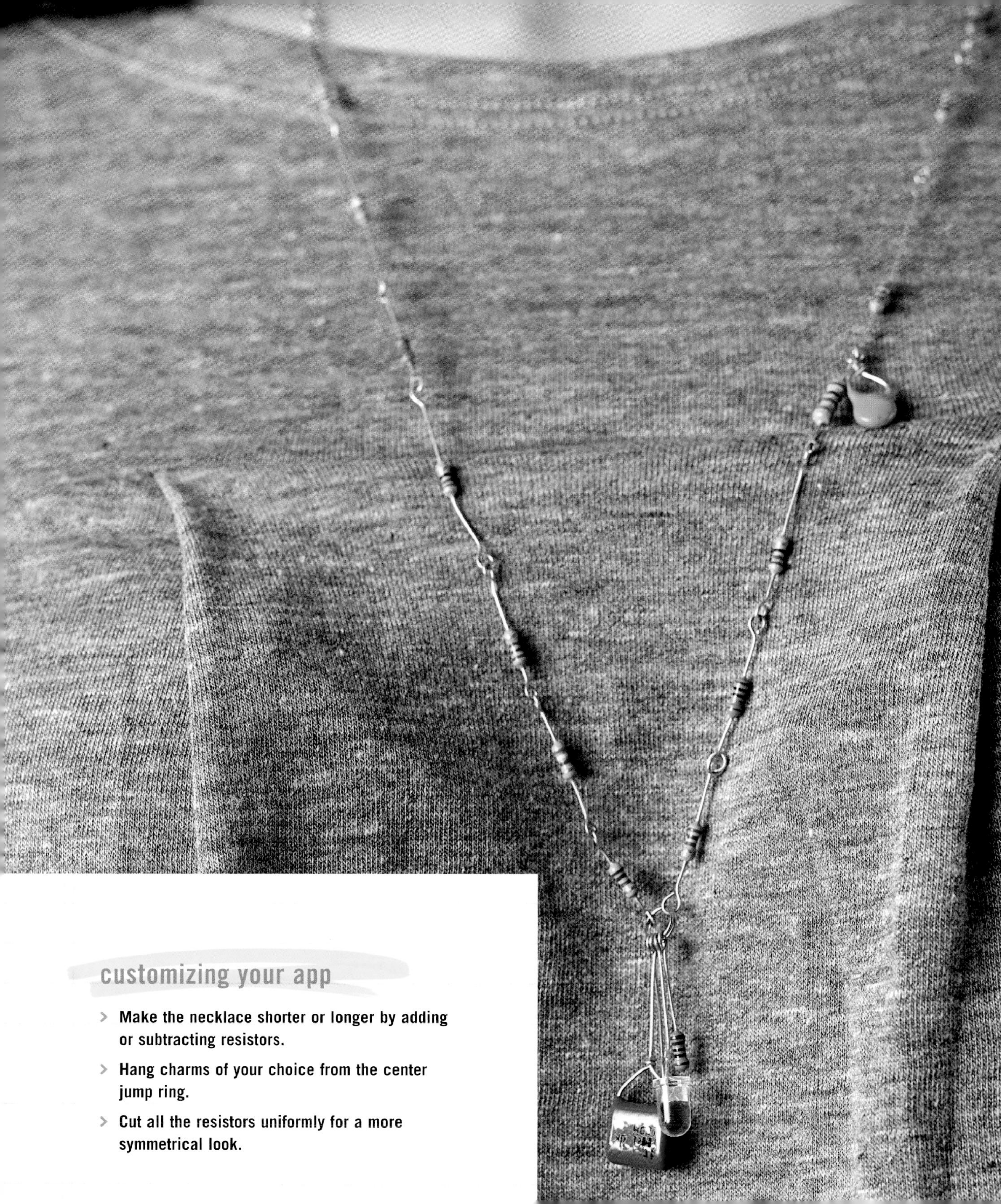

customizing your app

- Make the necklace shorter or longer by adding or subtracting resistors.
- Hang charms of your choice from the center jump ring.
- Cut all the resistors uniformly for a more symmetrical look.

{medium}

Digital Domain Bracelet

I love how versatile this bracelet is. The capacitors are like little blank slates, ready to be adapted for each of your friends. Put monograms on them to make them preppy. Draw private jokes on them for your best friend. Write things such as "LOL" or "OIC" on them for your favorite computer geek. You could easily make a whole batch and customize them for friends and family.

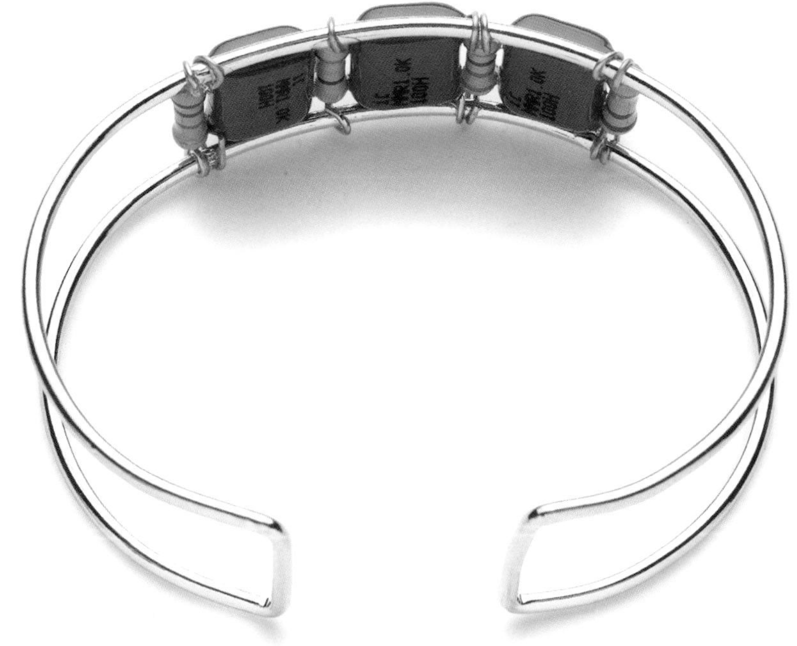

COMPONENTS AND HARDWARE

- 4 MEDIUM TAN RESISTORS {Radio Shack part number: 271-306}
- 3 MEDIUM ORANGE-BROWN CAPACITORS {Allied part number: 613-0546}
- 1 CUFF BRACELET FRAME
- ROUND-NOSE PLIERS
- WIRE CUTTERS
- SUPER GLUE OR JEWELRY GLUE
- MATERIALS TO DECORATE YOUR BRACELET, SUCH AS WATERPROOF PERMANENT MARKER, SWAROVSKI FLAT-BACK CRYSTALS, GLITTER NAIL POLISH, OR ANYTHING YOU CHOOSE

more

application

1. Take all of the resistors and three capacitors and trim each lead to about ½ inch (1.3 cm). Use round-nose pliers to loop the ends on each tan resistor. Test to see if the loops on your resistors fit around the bracelet frame and adjust the loops accordingly.

2. Hold each orange-brown capacitor so the printing is on the back and use round-nose pliers to bend the leads to the sides. Then loop each lead toward the back of the capacitor. Test to see if the loops fit around the bracelet frame and adjust the loops accordingly.

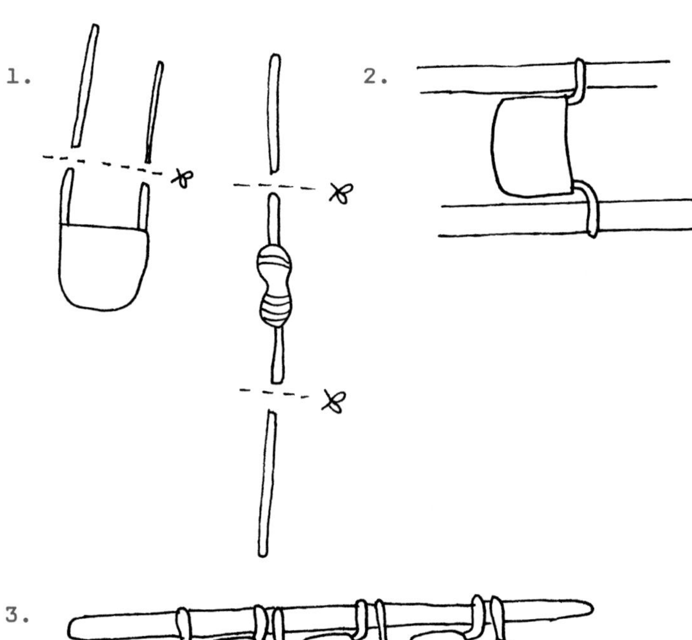

3. After the loops have been tested and adjusted, arrange the pieces on the bracelet frame in alternating order, starting and ending with resistors. Tighten all loops around the bracelet frame and use glue to secure the pieces together so they don't slide around.

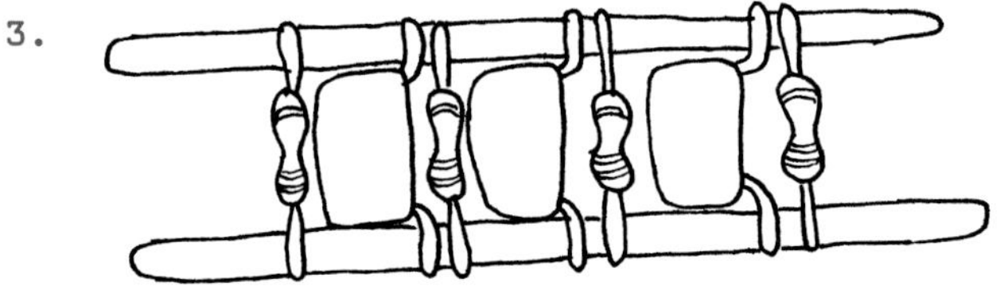

4. Personalize your bracelet! Draw pictures on the capacitors with a waterproof permanent marker, glue tiny Swarovski crystals onto the capacitors in the shapes of initials, decoupage tiny pictures from magazines or the Web, write a special message with glow-in-the-dark paint—use your imagination.

customizing your app

- **Use only capacitors or resistors.**
- **Fill up the entire bracelet frame with capacitors and resistors.**
- **Use various-size capacitors and resistors and change the order and configuration.**

TOP 10 LIST

WEBLOGS

1 boingboing.net
2 slashdot.org
3 engadget.com
4 lifehacker.com
5 radar.oreilly.com
6 gizmodo.com
7 neatorama.com
8 kotaku.com
9 alistapart.com
10 43folders.com

Digital Domain Bracelet? Check. Nerd-girl glasses? Check. All systems go for a day in the city.

Digital Domain Bracelet

{medium}

Link-Me-Up Necklace

This project is repetitive in a knitting-a-scarf kind of way—perfect for a rainy afternoon filled with movie watching. Before you know it, you will be cutting and looping these little resistors without taking your eyes off the screen.

COMPONENTS AND HARDWARE

> 30 MEDIUM TAN RESISTORS
{Radio Shack part number: 271-306}

> 1 SMALL TAN RESISTOR
{Radio Shack part number: 271-308}

> 4 4MM GREEN SWAROVSKI CRYSTAL BEADS

> JUMP RING OR SPRING RING

> 1 TOGGLE CLASP

> NEEDLE-NOSE PLIERS

> ROUND-NOSE PLIERS

> WIRE CUTTERS

more

application

1. Grab a handful of medium tan resistors and start trimming the leads to about ½ inch (1.3 cm) each. Then loop all the ends with round-nose pliers. I alternate trimming and looping because looping can strain your fingers after about ten minutes.

2. Make a chain out of the looped resistors (see page 25). Stop when the chain is 16 inches (40.6 cm) long.

3. Attach the toggle clasp components to the loops at both ends of the chain.

4. Take the small tan resistor and slide three green beads onto one lead. Trim the lead and loop the end to keep the beads from sliding off. Repeat with the remaining bead on the other lead. Attach the beaded resistor to the jump ring.

5. Attach the jump ring (with the beaded resistor attached) to the ring half of the toggle clasp.

2.

3.

4.

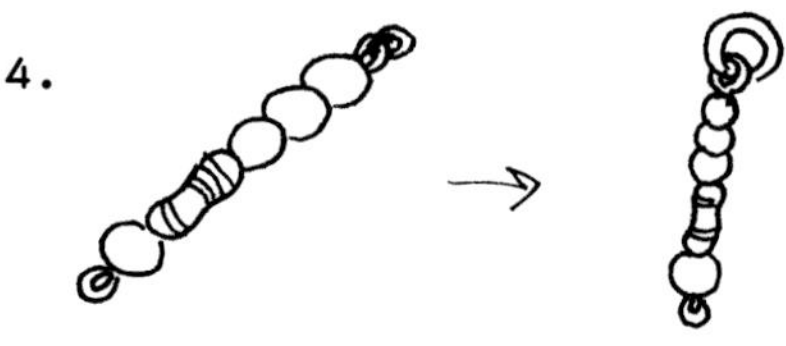

5.

customizing your app

> **Mix up large, medium, and small resistors in the chain.**

> **Attach a few capacitors onto the chain as charms.**

> **Slide a bead onto one lead of each resistor before clipping the leads and looping the ends (note that this will make your necklace longer in the end, so measure as you go).**

GEEK CITIES

1. San Francisco
2. Seattle
3. Austin
4. Los Angeles
5. Pittsburgh
6. Washington, D.C.
7. Raleigh-Durham
8. Orlando
9. Boston
10. New York City

You can do so much to customize this necklace, like adding beads or altering the length—ultimately it's the wearer who makes it truly unique.

{medium}

Digital Coral Necklace

This necklace was inspired by *The Little Mermaid*—one of my favorite movies. I love how the dangly parts move with you, and they look just like real coral!

COMPONENTS AND HARDWARE

- **20–25 SMALL BLUE RESISTORS** {Radio Shack part number: 271-309}
- **5 MEDIUM TAN RESISTORS** {Radio Shack part number: 271-1122}
- **25 SMALL TAN RESISTORS** {Radio Shack part number: 271-308}
- **1 TOGGLE CLASP**
- **NEEDLE-NOSE PLIERS**
- **ROUND-NOSE PLIERS**
- **WIRE CUTTERS**

more

application

1. Take all the tan resistors and trim all the leads to about ½ inch (1.3 cm). Then loop the ends with your round-nose pliers.

2. Chain all the tan resistors together (see page 25), randomly spacing the medium ones throughout. Stop when the chain is 18 inches (45.5 cm) long.

3. Fasten the toggle clasp components at each end of the chain.

4. Take the blue resistors and cut one lead completely off each one, then trim the remaining lead to about ½ inch (1.3 cm). Loop all the ends with round-nose pliers.

5. Make three "herringbone" chains with the blue resistors, following the pattern in the illustration. Be sure your loops are small enough that the resistors don't slide right through. I've suggested using 20 to 25 small blue resistors to divide into three herringbone chains; the final count is up to you.

6. Attach the longest herringbone blue chain at the exact center of your tan resistor chain. Position and attach the other two blue chains about 1½ inches (3.8 cm) apart on either side of the center.

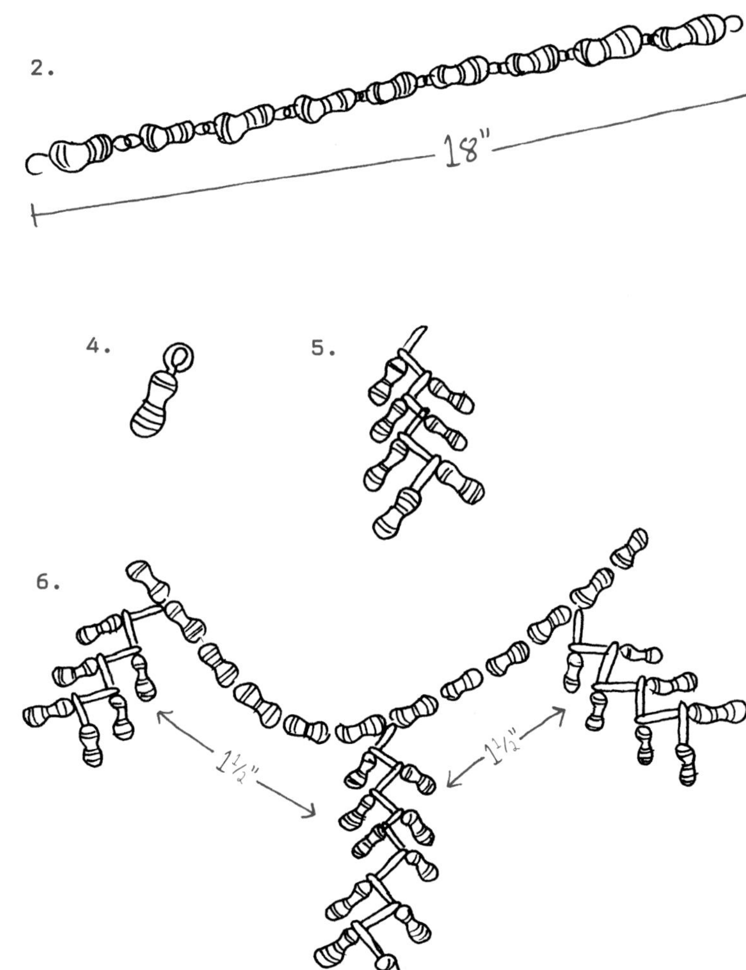

customizing your app

- Make the herringbone chains out of more tan resistors (instead of blue) for a more neutral look.
- Add a herringbone cluster every 1½ inches (3.8 cm) throughout the necklace.
- Attach only one herringbone cluster at the center, but make it super long.

TOP 10 LIST GEEK MOVIES

1 *Back to the Future* trilogy
2 *Sneakers*
3 *Star Wars*
4 *Dr. Strangelove*
5 *Pi*
6 *The Hitchhiker's Guide to the Galaxy*
7 *Lord of the Rings* trilogy
8 *Real Genius*
9 *Office Space*
10 *The Fifth Element*

Shanaé gives the Digital Coral Necklace a glimmer of glam by pairing it with a deep purple shirt.

Katie keeps it casual and cute at the park.

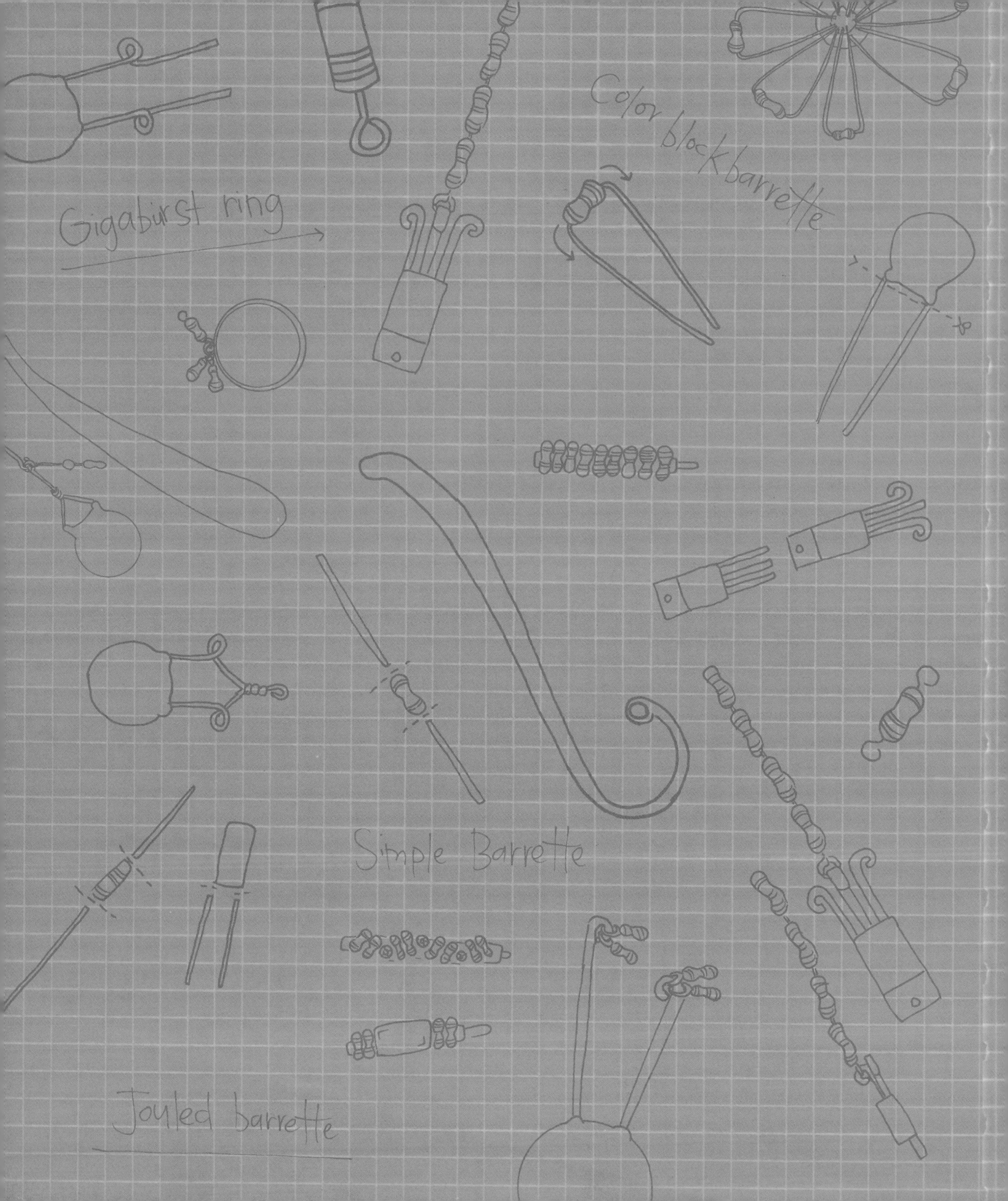
Gigaburst ring
Color block barrette
Simple Barrette
Jouled barrette

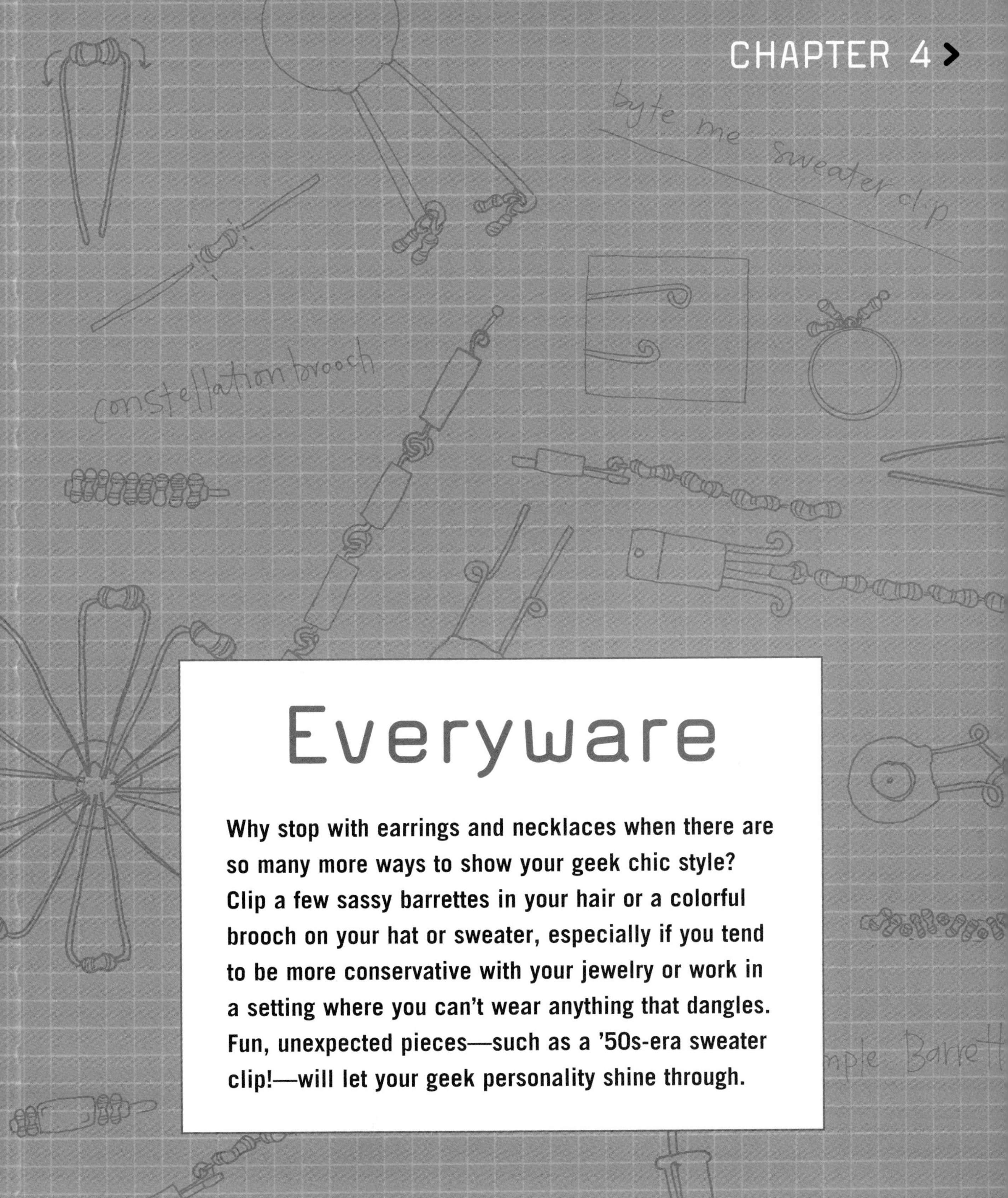

CHAPTER 4

Everyware

Why stop with earrings and necklaces when there are so many more ways to show your geek chic style? Clip a few sassy barrettes in your hair or a colorful brooch on your hat or sweater, especially if you tend to be more conservative with your jewelry or work in a setting where you can't wear anything that dangles. Fun, unexpected pieces—such as a '50s-era sweater clip!—will let your geek personality shine through.

{easy}

Gigaburst Ring

Do you ever talk with your hands? Now you can emphasize your point even better with the Gigaburst Ring. A gaggle of resistors at the top provides a shower of color for whatever hand you wear it on.

application

1. Trim the leads on all the resistors to about ½ inch (1.3 cm). Loop both ends with round-nose pliers.

1.

2. Begin attaching the looped resistors to the loops on your ring base. You can stop once you've filled up the loops, or keep going and attach resistors onto other resistors. I trimmed some of the excess bottom loops off the resistors, just for something a little different.

2.

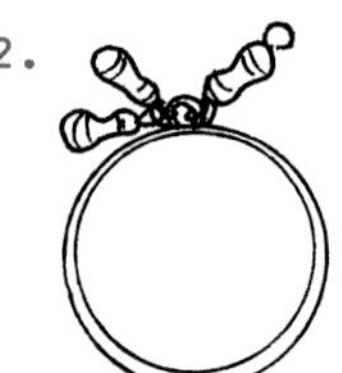

COMPONENTS AND HARDWARE

- **13–15 SMALL TAN RESISTORS** {Radio Shack part number: 271-308}
- **3 SMALL BLUE RESISTORS** {Radio Shack part number: 271-309}
- **1 RING WITH LOOPS** {available at jewelry and beading stores}
- **NEEDLE-NOSE PLIERS**
- **ROUND-NOSE PLIERS**
- **WIRE CUTTERS**

customizing your app

- **Attach small capacitors as well as resistors onto the ring loops.**
- **Add a bead to each resistor to boost the flash factor.**
- **Wrap colored jewelry wire around the base of the ring for a fun shot of color.**

Gigaburst ring

{easy}

Barrettes

Do you know what I really hate? When I'm concentrating on a project and I have to keep brushing my hair out of my eyes. It can drive you crazy, right? These barrettes not only keep your hair out of the way and thus keep you productive, but they also look girly and fun. Here are three super-easy versions.

COMPONENTS AND HARDWARE

- **10–13 SMALL TAN RESISTORS** {Radio Shack part number: 271-308}
- **1 SMALL BLUE RESISTOR** {Radio Shack part number: 271-309}
- **1 BAR BARRETTE**
- **NEEDLE-NOSE PLIERS OR TWEEZERS**
- **WIRE CUTTERS**
- **SUPER GLUE OR JEWELRY GLUE**

Simple Barrette

application

1. Cut both leads completely off enough tan and blue resistors to cover the whole top of the barrette (I needed eleven resistors for mine).

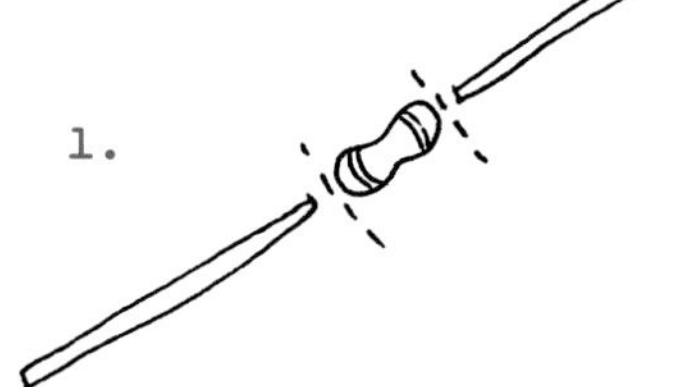

2. Gently glue each resistor onto the bar. Randomly add the blue resistor for a bit of contrast! Let dry for at least an hour.

Simple Barrette

more

Color Block Barrette

application

1. Cut both leads completely off all the capacitors and resistors.

2. Glue the pieces to the barrette in this order: two tan resistors, the blue capacitor, two tan resistors. Let dry for at least an hour.

1.

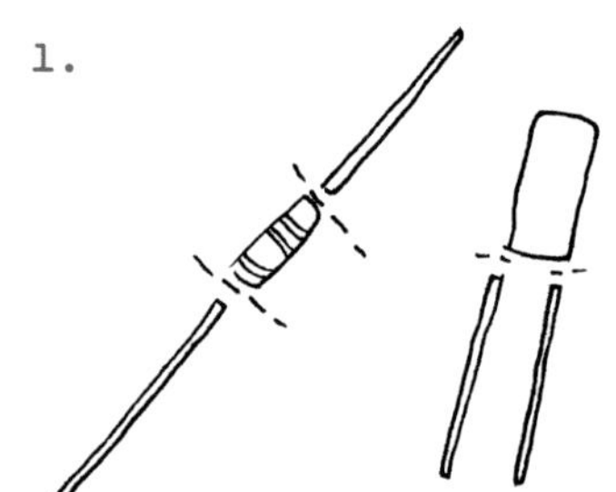

2.

Color block barrette

COMPONENTS AND HARDWARE

- **4 MEDIUM TAN RESISTORS** {Radio Shack part number: 271-1122}
- **1 MEDIUM BLUE CAPACITOR** {Radio Shack part number: 272-1053}
- **1 BAR BARRETTE**
- **NEEDLE-NOSE PLIERS OR TWEEZERS**
- **WIRE CUTTERS**
- **SUPER GLUE OR JEWELRY GLUE**

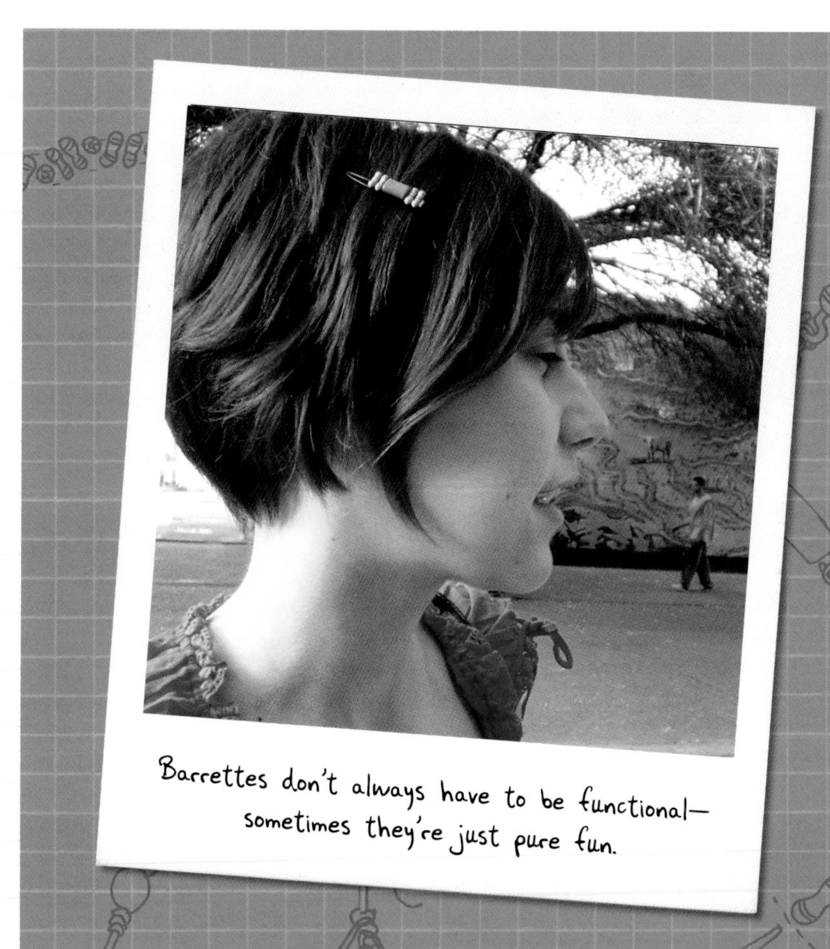

Barrettes don't always have to be functional—sometimes they're just pure fun.

Jouled Barrette

application

1. Cut both leads completely off an even number of tan resistors.

2. Arrange and glue two resistors side by side at a 45-degree angle. Then glue two more facing opposite the first two, as shown. Continue the pattern to the end of the barrette.

3. Using needle-nose pliers or tweezers, carefully glue the Swarovski crystals in the little spaces left uncovered by the resistors. Let dry for at least an hour.

1.

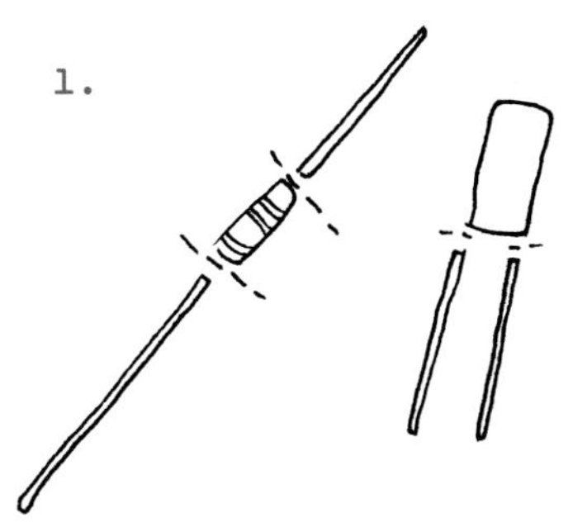

3.

COMPONENTS AND HARDWARE

- **8–10 SMALL TAN RESISTORS** {Radio Shack part number: 271-308}
- **3 10SS XILION SWAROVSKI FLAT-BACK CRYSTALS**
- **1 BAR BARRETTE**
- **NEEDLE-NOSE PLIERS OR TWEEZERS**
- **WIRE CUTTERS**
- **SUPER GLUE OR JEWELRY GLUE**

Jouled barrette

customizing your apps

- **Reverse the Simple Barrette color scheme and use one tan and twelve blue resistors.**
- **Add more jewels on top of the resistors.**
- **Use a herringbone or checkerboard pattern on the barrettes.**

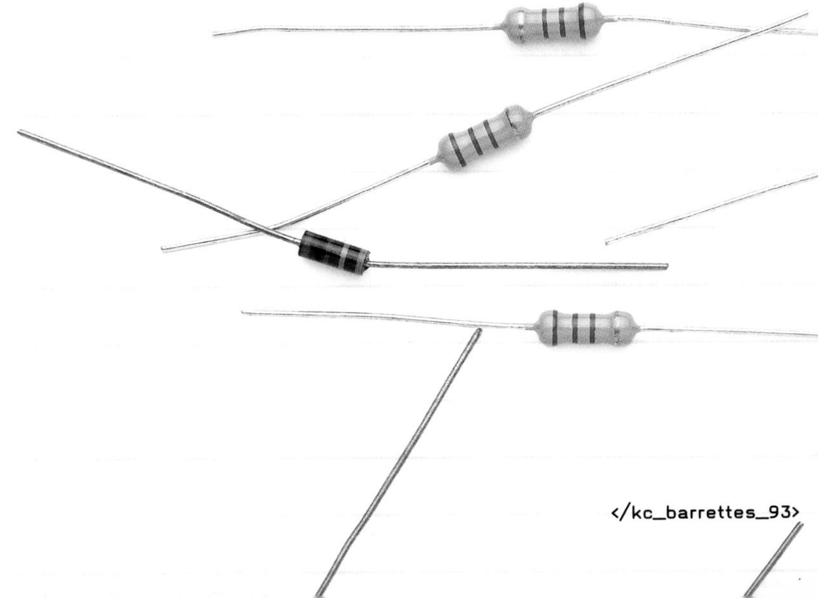

{medium}

Brooches

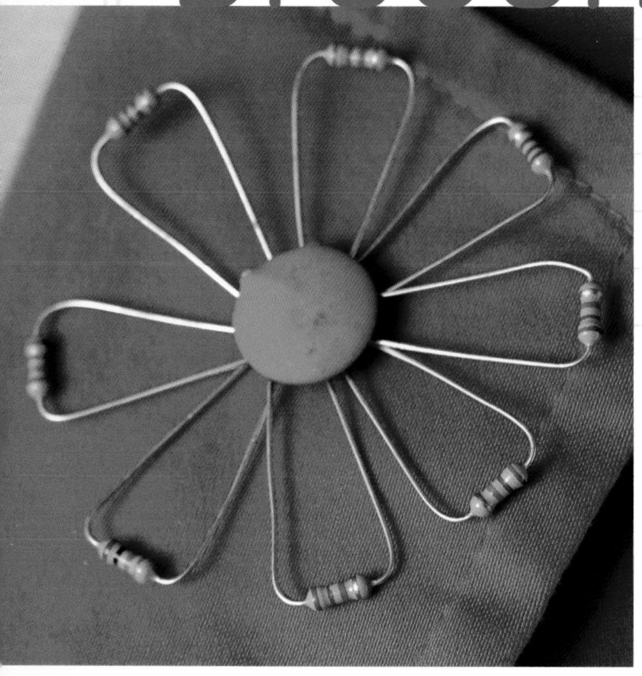

Brooches are one of my most favorite types of jewelry. I wear a light jacket or sweater every day, and what better way to add some personal style than a unique, DIY brooch? These are especially great if you don't really like wearing earrings or necklaces.

Floppy Flower Brooch

COMPONENTS AND HARDWARE

- 1 MEDIUM ORANGE CAPACITOR {Radio Shack part number: 272-131}
- 8 SMALL TAN RESISTORS {Radio Shack part number: 271-308}
- 1 PIN BACK
- NEEDLE-NOSE PLIERS
- ROUND-NOSE PLIERS
- WIRE CUTTERS
- SUPER GLUE OR JEWELRY GLUE

more

application

1. Fold both leads on each tan resistor into a U shape.

2. Take the orange capacitor and cut both leads completely off.

3. Lay the capacitor on a flat surface with the text side up. Dab a bit of glue on the capacitor and glue down the leads of a resistor to make the first petal. Repeat for the remaining seven petals. Let dry thoroughly.

4. Add a large dot of glue on the text side of the capacitor and attach the pin back. Let dry.

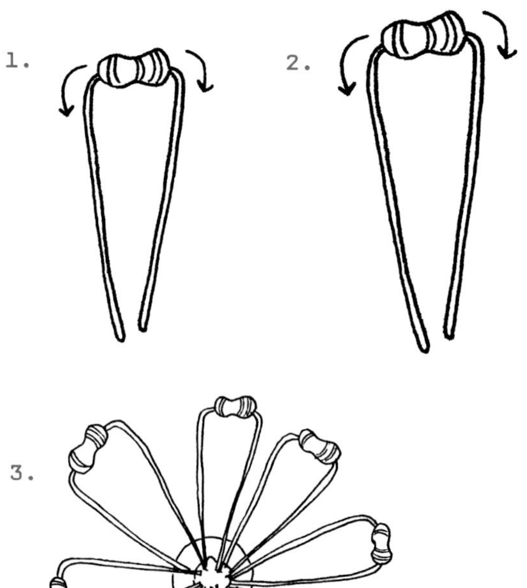

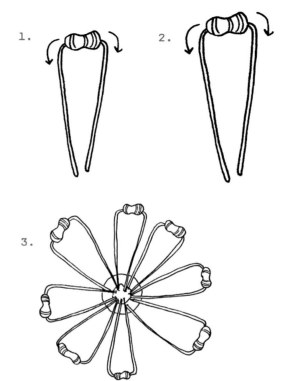

Wearing the Floppy Flower Brooch is like wearing a smiley face button—it just exudes happy vibes!

Constellation Brooch

application

1. Take your blue resistor or large capacitor and clip off a tiny bit of one lead, enough to make the leads uneven, and then use round-nose pliers to round both ends to face each other.

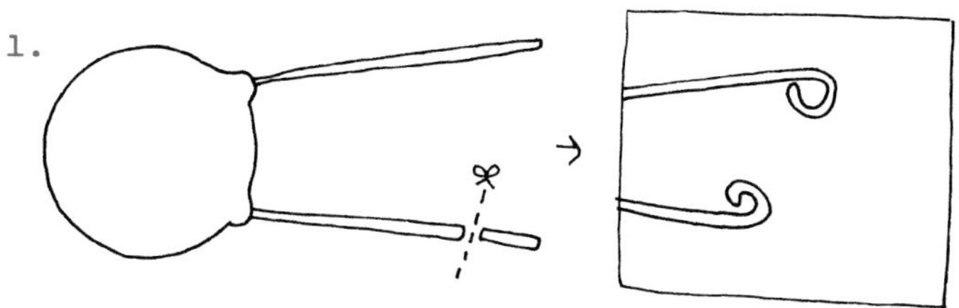

2. Cut one lead completely off each of the resistors and trim the remaining ends to about ½ inch (1.3 cm). Loop the ends.

2.

3. Attach the resistors to the loops on the capacitor's leads.

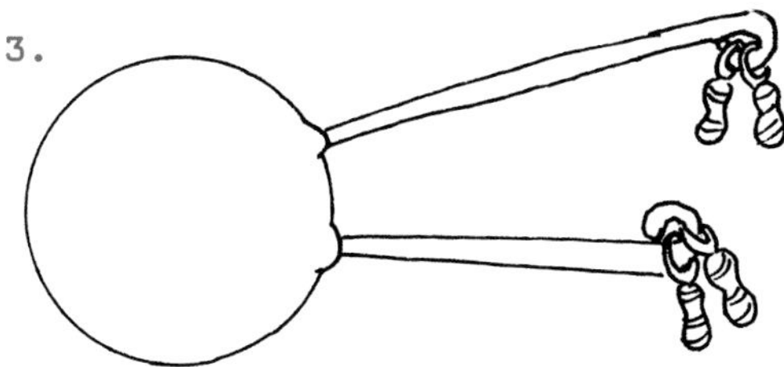

4. Glue the eleven Swarovski crystals randomly onto the body of the capacitor. Let dry thoroughly.

5. Glue the pin back onto the reverse side. Let dry.

COMPONENTS AND HARDWARE

- BLUE METAL-OXIDE VARISTOR {Radio Shack part number: 276-568} or any large capacitor
- 4 SMALL TAN RESISTORS {Radio Shack part number: 271-308}
- 1 SMALL BLUE RESISTOR {Radio Shack part number: 271-309}
- 11 5SS XILION SWAROVSKI FLAT-BACK CRYSTALS
- 1 PIN BACK
- NEEDLE-NOSE PLIERS
- ROUND-NOSE PLIERS
- WIRE CUTTERS
- SUPER GLUE OR JEWELRY GLUE

constellation brooch

customizing your apps

- **Cover the blue varistor completely in Swarovski crystals.**
- **Add more "petals" to the Floppy Flower Brooch.**
- **Hang small capacitors from the loops on the blue varistor.**

{medium}

Sweater Clips

Sweater clips aren't very common anymore, but in the 1950s and 1960s they were essential accessories for every lady, as they're used to keep a sweater fastened when it is draped around your shoulders. My grandmother used to wear sweater clips in her youth, and I just think they are too neat and ready for a comeback!

Open-Source Sweater Clip

COMPONENTS AND HARDWARE

- **2 MEDIUM ORANGE CAPACITORS** {Radio Shack part number: 272-131}
- **6 SMALL TAN RESISTORS** {Radio Shack part number: 271-308}
- **2 PIN BACKS**
- **NEEDLE-NOSE PLIERS**
- **ROUND-NOSE PLIERS**
- **WIRE CUTTERS**
- **SUPER GLUE OR JEWELRY GLUE**

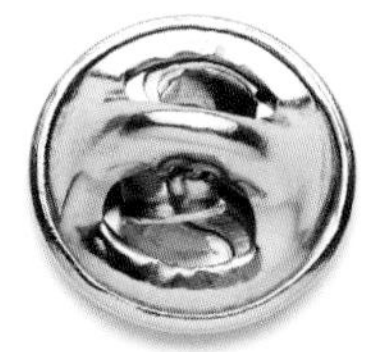

more

application

1. Begin with the orange capacitors. Carefully twist each lead into a loop, as shown, so the loop is in the middle.

2. Now do the capacitor wrap (see page 26) using the straight portion of the leads below the loop. Position the end loop perpendicular to the body of the capacitor.

3. Take the tan resistors and trim all the leads to ½ inch (1.3 cm). Use round-nose pliers to loop the ends. Then chain the six resistors together (see page 25).

4. Connect a capacitor to each end of the chain by the end loop.

5. Finish up by gluing a pin back onto the reverse of each capacitor. Let dry thoroughly. You can also do this step before attaching the resistor chain.

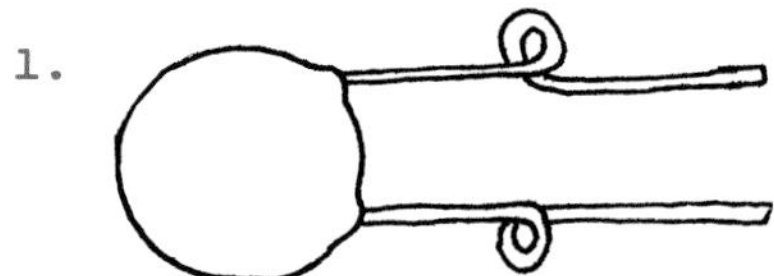

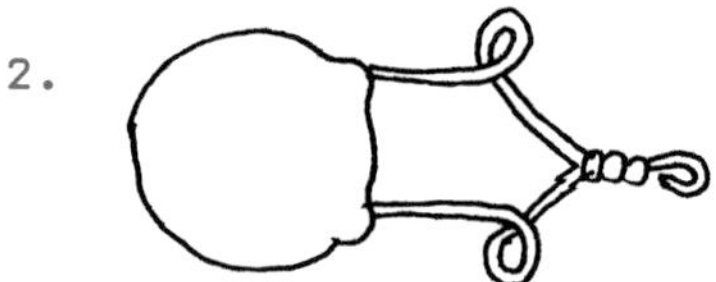

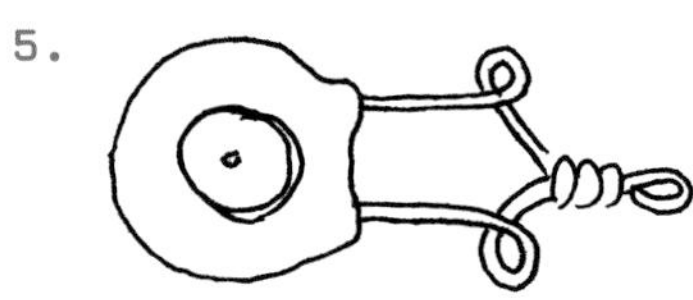

Byte Me Sweater Clip

application

1. Take the two voltage regulators and use round-nose pliers to loop the three prongs. The outer loops should face outward; the center loop should be perpendicular to the body of the voltage regulator.

1.

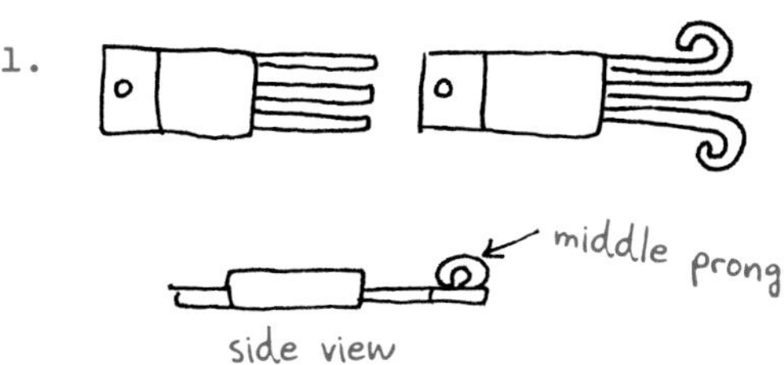

2. Clip the leads of all the blue resistors to about ½ inch (1.3 cm) and loop the ends. Chain the resistors together (see page 25), and then attach each end to the center loop on each voltage regulator.

2.

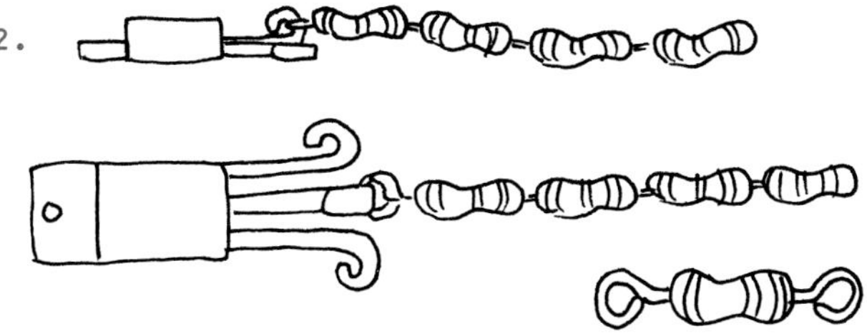

3. Glue a pin back to the reverse of each voltage regulator. Let dry thoroughly. You can also do this step before attaching the resistor chain.

customizing your app

> **Glue Swarovski crystals onto the bases of the sweater clips.**

> **Make your sweater clips super long or super short, depending on the number of resistors you chain together.**

> **Connect resistors to the extra loops on the base pieces of the voltage regulators for a little added movement.**

COMPONENTS AND HARDWARE

> **2 VOLTAGE REGULATORS** {Radio Shack part number: 276-1771}

> **6 SMALL BLUE RESISTORS** {Radio Shack part number: 272-1053}

> **2 PIN BACKS**

> **NEEDLE-NOSE PLIERS**

> **ROUND-NOSE PLIERS**

> **WIRE CUTTERS**

> **SUPER GLUE OR JEWELRY GLUE**

byte me sweater clip

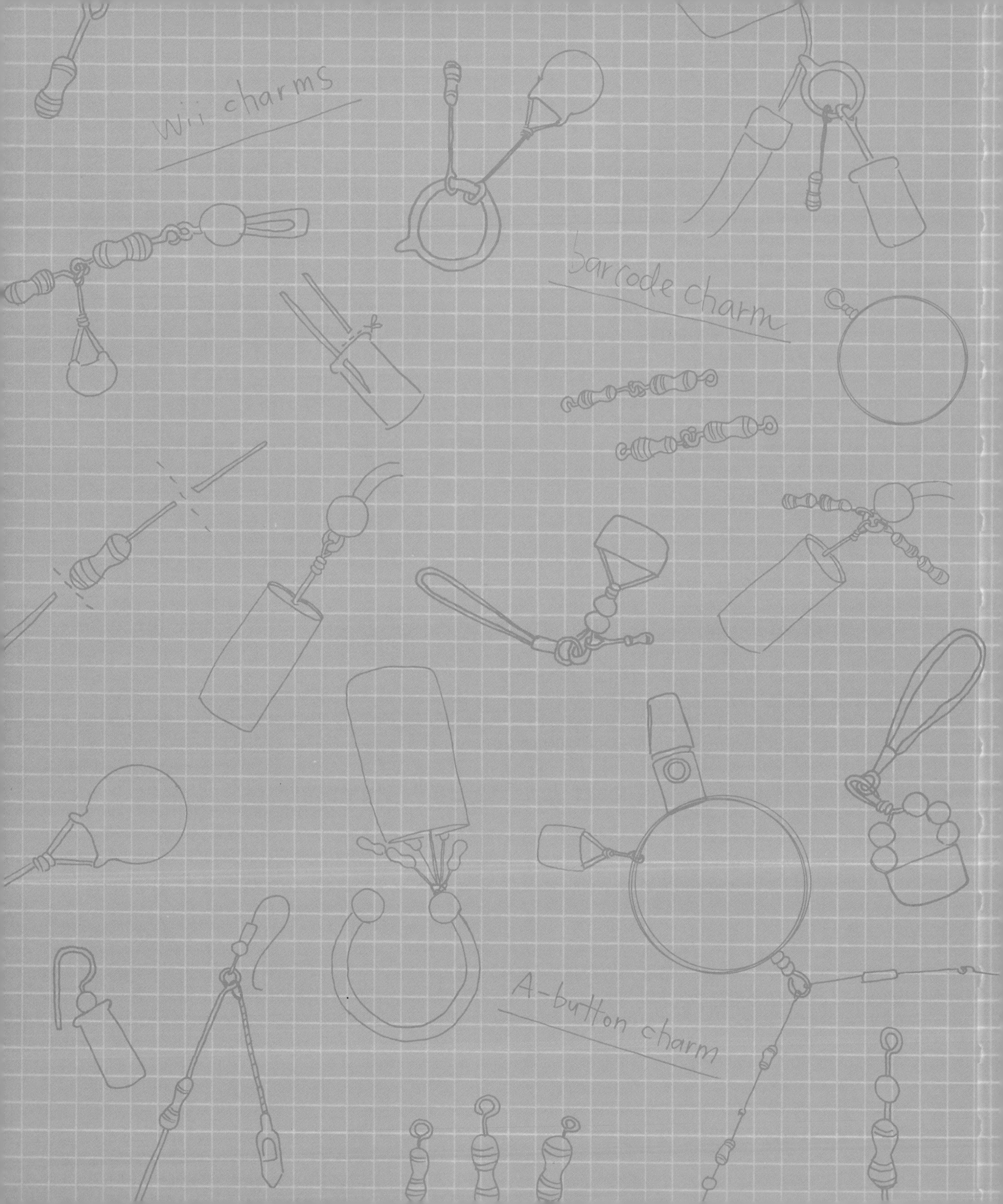
Wii charms
barcode charm
A-button charm

CHAPTER 5

Geekery and Gifts

What better way to share your passion for all things geek chic than to gift loved ones with your handmade inspirations? The projects in this chapter are perfect for those friends and family members who have everything and are just begging for something extra unique, such as bookmarks, key rings, and Wii charms. From gamers to bookworms to cell phone addicts, these projects will have your gift needs covered.

{easy}

Wii Charms

My sister and I love to play the Nintendo Wii, but we always get our Wiimotes confused. So I came up with these charms to attach to each Wiimote so we can tell ours apart. The key is to make the charms fairly short so they won't swing around wildly during game play.

A-button charm

COMPONENTS AND HARDWARE

- 1 BLACK CAPACITOR {Allied part number: 852-7000}
- 1 SMALL TAN RESISTOR {Radio Shack part number: 271-308}
- 1 TOGGLE CLASP OR LARGE JUMP RING
- NEEDLE-NOSE PLIERS
- ROUND-NOSE PLIERS
- WIRE CUTTERS

more

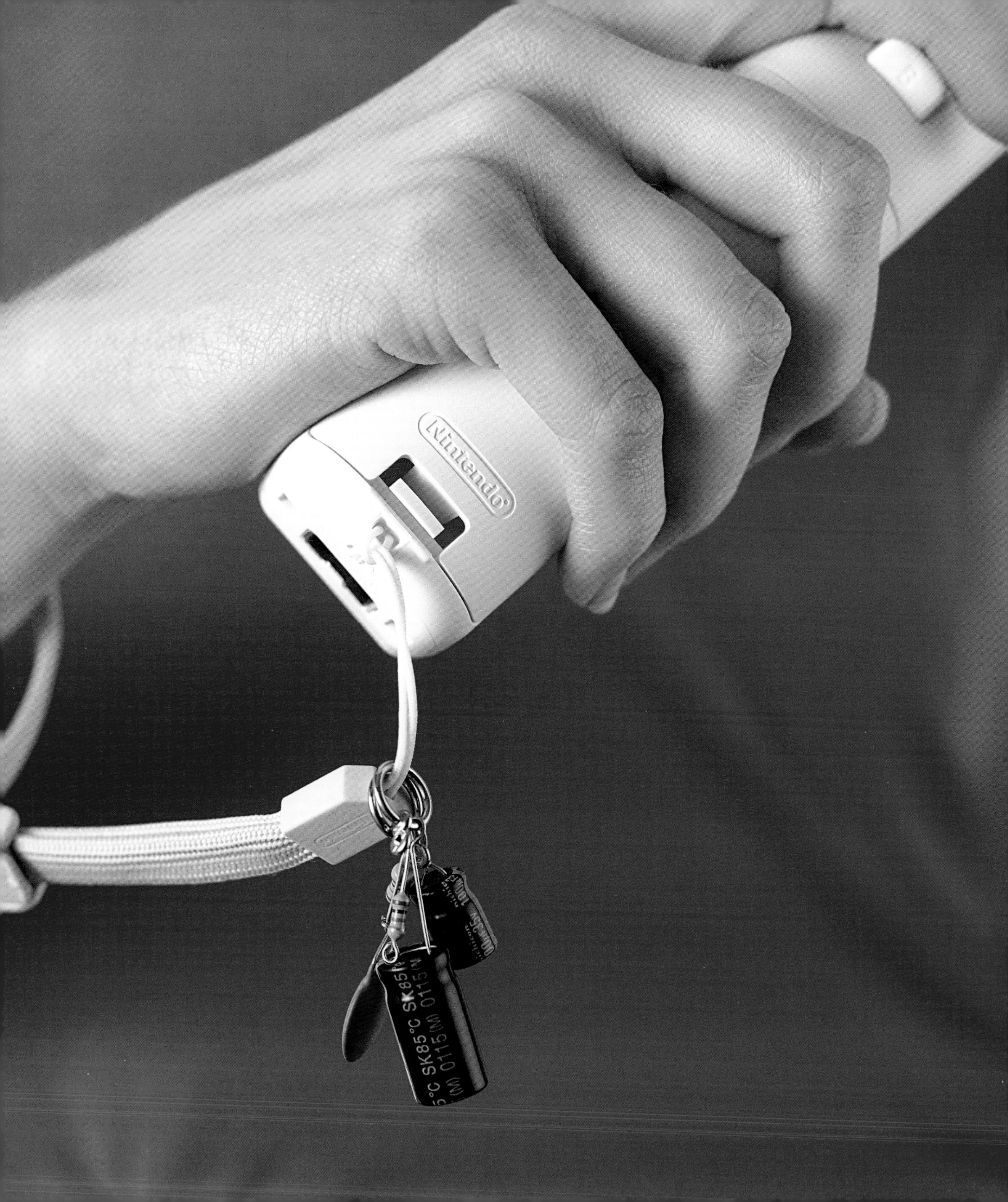
Nintendo
SK85°C
0115(M)

application

1. Take the black capacitor and cut one lead completely off. Then loop the end of the remaining lead with round-nose pliers. Attach the loop to the jump ring or ring half of the toggle clasp.

2. Cut one lead completely off the tan resistor. Trim the other lead to about ½ inch (1.3 cm). Loop the end and attach it to the same jump ring.

3. Attach the jump ring to the string that connects your Wiimote to its strap.

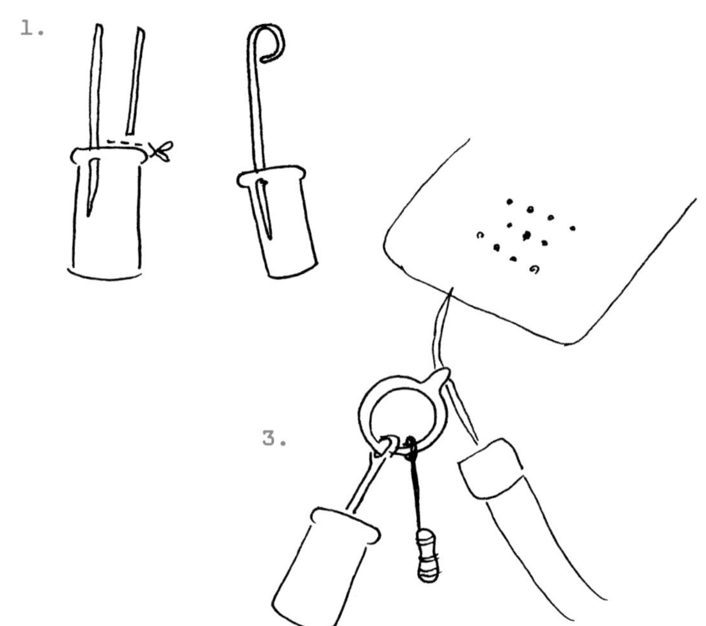

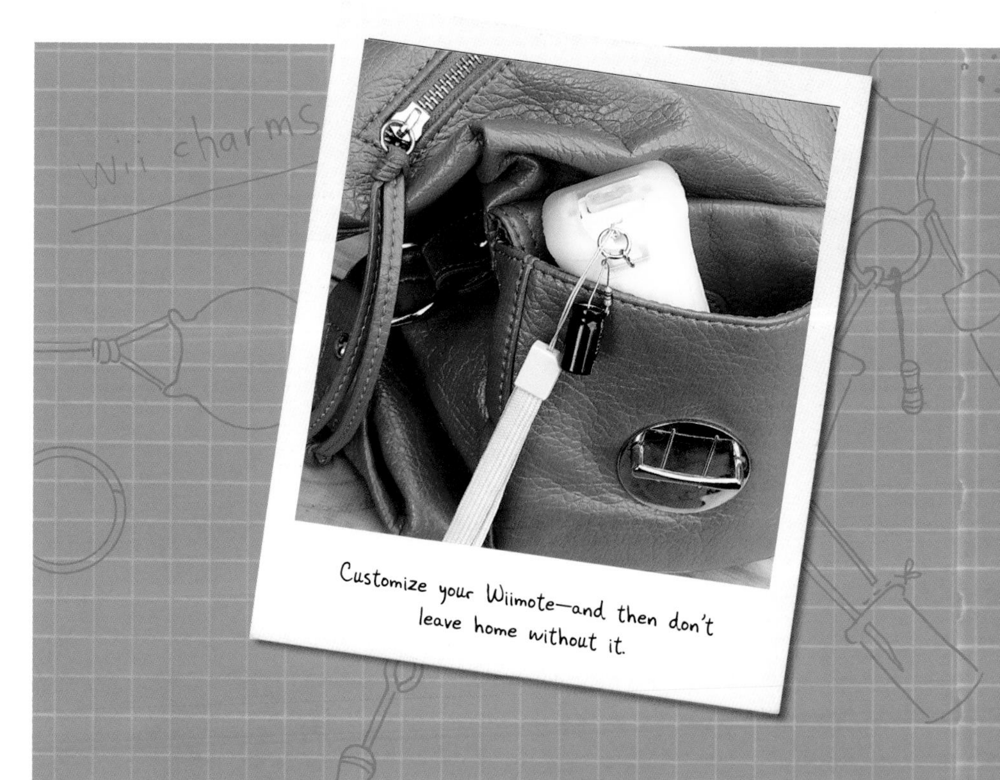

Customize your Wiimote—and then don't leave home without it.

B-Button Charm

application

1. Take the blue capacitor and orange capacitor and perform the capacitor wrap on each (see page 26). Then loop the ends of the leads with round-nose pliers. Attach the loops to the jump ring or ring half of the toggle clasp.

2. Cut one lead completely off the tan resistor. Trim the other lead to about ½ inch (1.3 cm). Loop the end. Attach this to the jump ring as well.

3. Attach the jump ring to the string that connects your Wiimote to its strap.

- **1 MEDIUM BLUE CAPACITOR** {Radio Shack part number: 272-1028}
- **1 MEDIUM ORANGE CAPACITOR** {Radio Shack part number: 272-131}
- **1 SMALL TAN RESISTOR** {Radio Shack part number: 271-308}
- **1 TOGGLE CLASP OR JUMP RING**
- **NEEDLE-NOSE PLIERS**
- **ROUND-NOSE PLIERS**
- **WIRE CUTTERS**

customizing your app

- **Add beads or charms related to your favorite video games.**
- **Decorate the capacitors with paint pens or waterproof permanent markers.**
- **Add Swarovski crystals to give your charms an upscale touch.**

{easy}

Bitmap Bookmark

Chances are, if you are a nerd, you are also a bookworm. And even a bookworm has to take a break sometime. What better way to pause in your reading than with some techie book jewelry?

COMPONENTS AND HARDWARE

- **1 ORANGE CERAMIC DISC CAPACITOR** {Radio Shack part number: 272-135}
- **1 MEDIUM GREEN CAPACITOR** {Radio Shack part number: 272-1070}
- **1 SMALL BLUE RESISTOR** {Radio Shack part number: 272-1053}
- **1 MEDIUM TAN RESISTOR** {Radio Shack part number: 271-1122}
- **1 4MM GREEN SWAROVSKI BEAD**
- **1 STAINLESS STEEL OR STERLING SILVER BOOKMARK**
- **NEEDLE-NOSE PLIERS**
- **ROUND-NOSE PLIERS**
- **WIRE CUTTERS**

application

1. Take the two capacitors and do a capacitor wrap on each (see page 26).

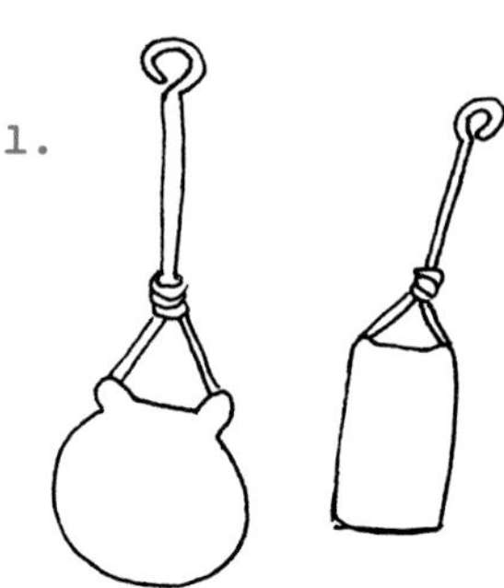

2. Take the medium tan resistor and trim one lead to ½ inch (1.3 cm). Trim the other lead to about 1 inch (2.5 cm). Loop both ends.

3. Take the small blue resistor and cut one lead completely off. Trim the other lead to about 1 inch (2.5 cm). Slide a green bead onto the lead, then use round-nose pliers to loop the end.

4. Attach the tan resistor and orange capacitor to the hole in the bookmark. Attach the blue resistor and green capacitor to the bottom loop of the tan resistor.

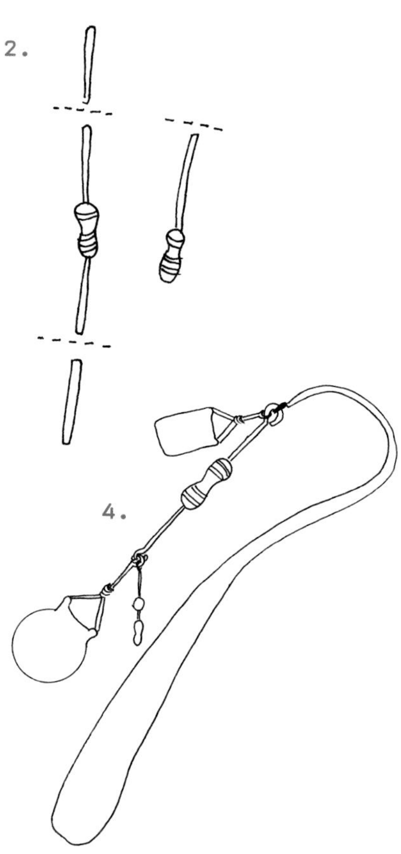

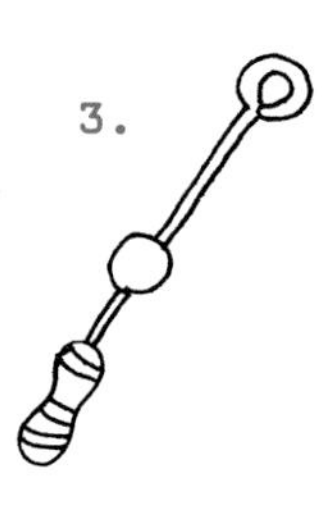

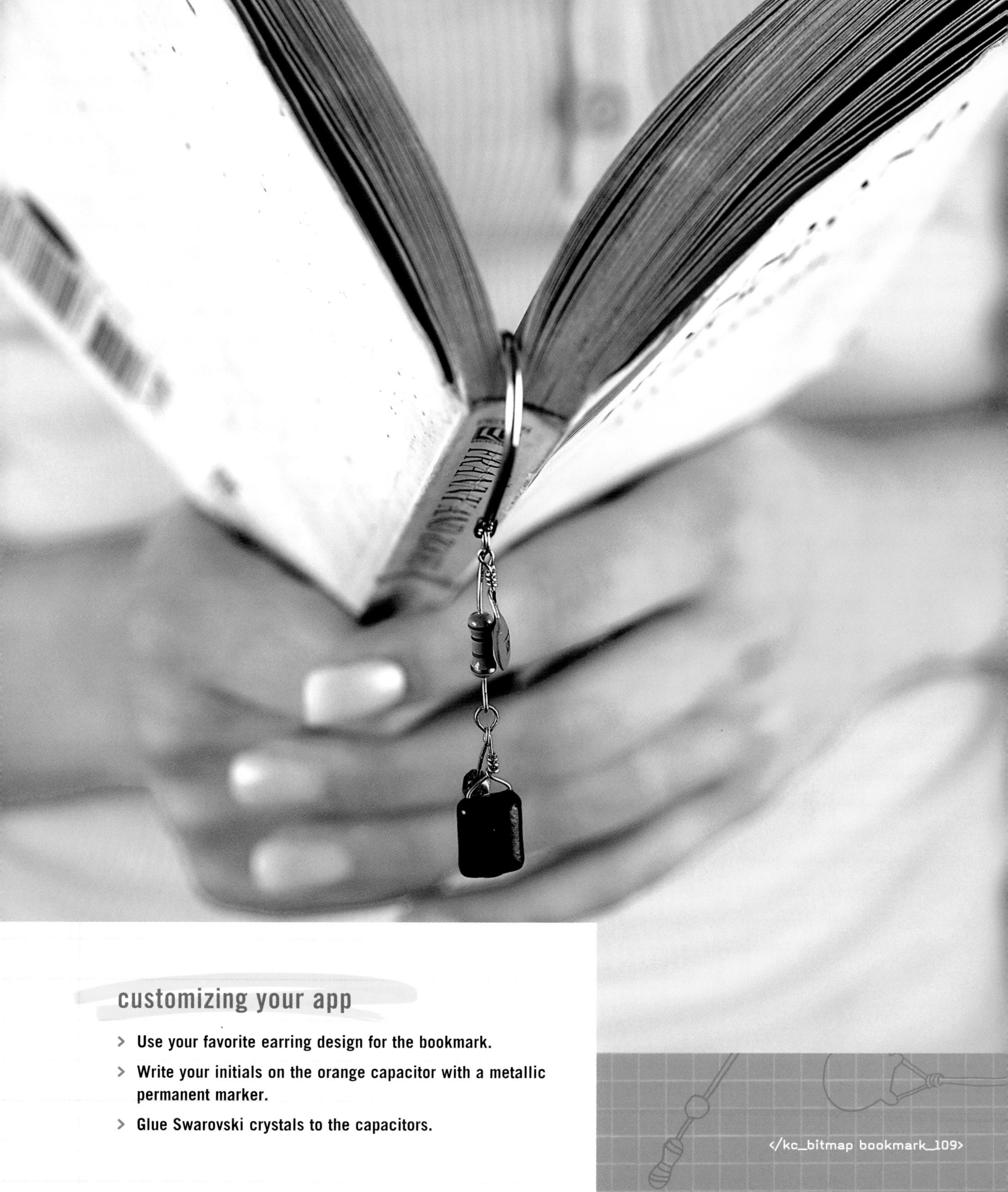

customizing your app

- Use your favorite earring design for the bookmark.
- Write your initials on the orange capacitor with a metallic permanent marker.
- Glue Swarovski crystals to the capacitors.

{easy}

Key Ring

I hate when one of my friends is having a bad day, so I usually try to make him or her a useful little pick-me-up. Key chains are a great unisex gift, perfect for almost anybody. Five-year-olds collect them, and your best friend probably needs one for her mailbox or bike key.

COMPONENTS AND HARDWARE

- **1 LARGE BLUE CAPACITOR** {Radio Shack part number: 242-1047}
- **1 MEDIUM TAN RESISTOR** {Radio Shack part number: 271-1106}
- **4 SMALL TAN RESISTORS** {Radio Shack part number: 271-308}
- **1 HORSESHOE-SHAPED KEY RING WITH LOOP**
- **NEEDLE-NOSE PLIERS**
- **ROUND-NOSE PLIERS**
- **WIRE CUTTERS**

more

nichicon

application

1. Take the blue capacitor and thread one lead through the hole in the key chain and wrap as in a capacitor wrap (see page 26). If your key chain doesn't have a hole, just wrap the lead around the main ring securely.

2. Trim all the leads on the four small tan resistors to ½ inch (1.3 cm) and then loop all the ends.

3. Make two chains of small resistors, two in each chain (see page 25). Attach the two chains to the main loop of the key ring.

4. Cut one lead completely off the medium tan resistor. Trim the other lead to about 1 inch (2.5 cm) and loop the end. Then attach it to the main key chain loop.

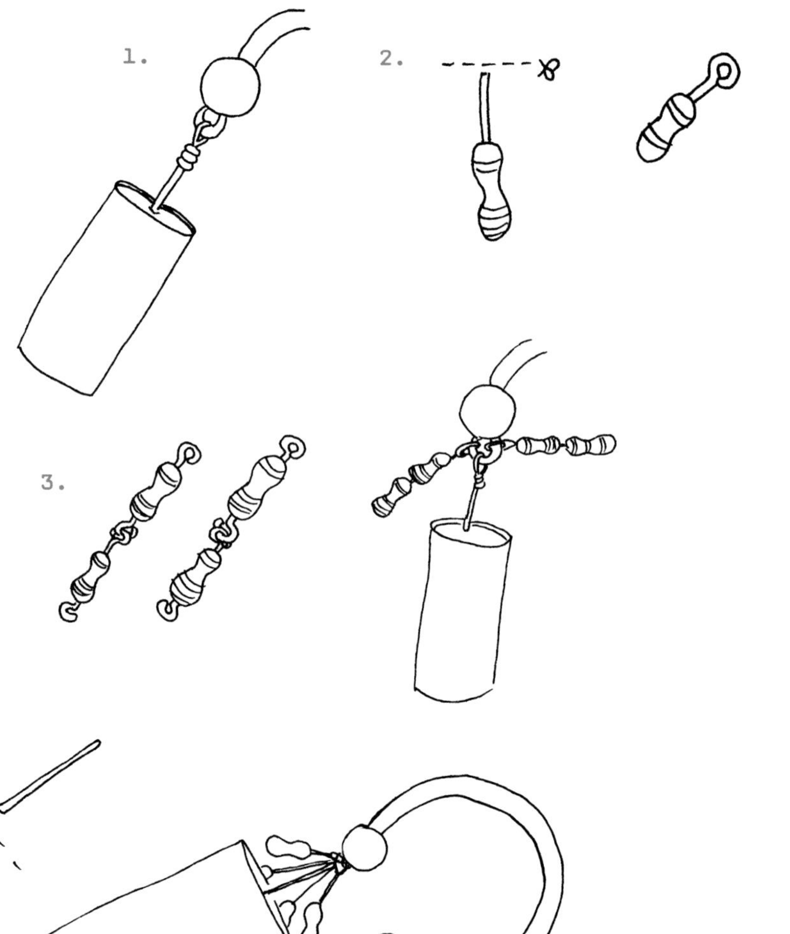

customizing your app

- **Glue a little ribbon around the main capacitor.**
- **Use a metallic marker or paint pen to add your friend's monogram or initials.**
- **Use this project as a stash-buster: Attach any remaining parts you have lying around to the key chain.**

TOP 10 LIST NERDY ACCESSORIES

1. Ironic/obscure T-shirt
2. Converse Chuck Taylor's or Vans
3. Laptop
4. Laptop bag plastered with 1-inch message pins
5. Cell phone/Smartphone
6. Digital watch
7. Planner/Palm PDA
8. Funky headband
9. Dark jeans
10. More message pins

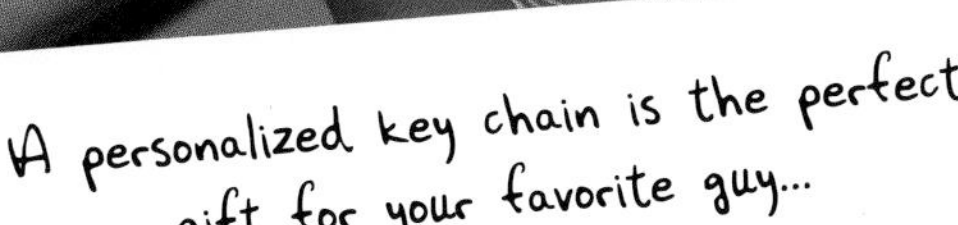

A personalized key chain is the perfect gift for your favorite guy...

...the dark blue capacitor gives it just the right masculine, gadgety edge.

{easy}

Celly Charms

Cell phones used to be a nerd status symbol, but now everybody and their dog has one, so your best bet to keep your phone original and show geek pride is with these cell phone charms. They are super easy to make and can be used as party favors. You can also convert them to wineglass charms by attaching them to a stemware hoop or hoop earring instead of to the jump ring.

COMPONENTS AND HARDWARE

- 1 SMALL TAN RESISTOR {Radio Shack part number: 271-308}
- 1 BLUE METALIZED FILM CAPACITOR {Radio Shack part number: 272-1053}
- 1 4MM GREEN SWAROVSKI BEAD
- 1 4MM YELLOW SWAROVSKI BEAD
- 1 JUMP RING
- NEEDLE-NOSE PLIERS
- ROUND-NOSE PLIERS
- WIRE CUTTERS

Blue Chip Charm

application

1. Take the blue capacitor and do the capacitor wrap (see page 26). Slide the two beads onto the lead. Then trim the lead and make a loop big enough to keep the beads from sliding off.

2. Take the tan resistor and cut one lead completely off. Trim the other lead to about ½ inch (1.3 cm). Loop the end.

3. Attach the resistor to the capacitor loop, then slide the beaded capacitor onto a jump ring.

1.

2.

3.

more

Mr. Roboto Charm

application

1. Take your black capacitor and do a basic capacitor wrap (see page 26). Slide the two beads onto the lead over the wrap. Then trim and loop the end.

2. Attach the charm to the jump ring.

mr. roboto

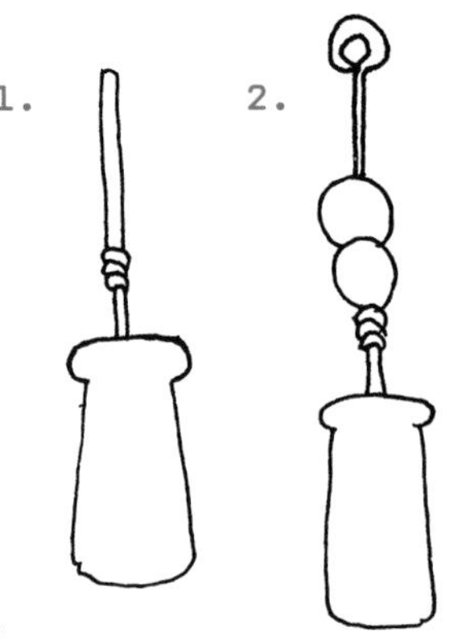

COMPONENTS AND HARDWARE

- 1 BLACK CAPACITOR {Allied part number: 852-7000}
- 1 4MM GREEN SWAROVSKI BEAD
- 1 4MM BLACK SWAROVSKI BEAD
- 1 JUMP RING
- NEEDLE-NOSE PLIERS
- ROUND-NOSE PLIERS
- WIRE CUTTERS

CD-ROM Charm

application

1. Cut one lead completely off the blue capacitor. Then slide the Swarovski bead onto the other lead.

2. Wrap the lead above the bead around something small, like a pencil, to form a bigger loop. Then wrap the rest of the lead around itself at the base of the loop.

3. Slide the charm off the pencil and attach it to the jump ring.

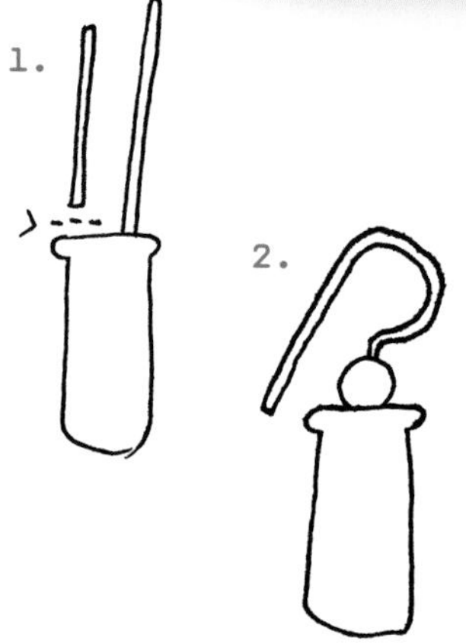

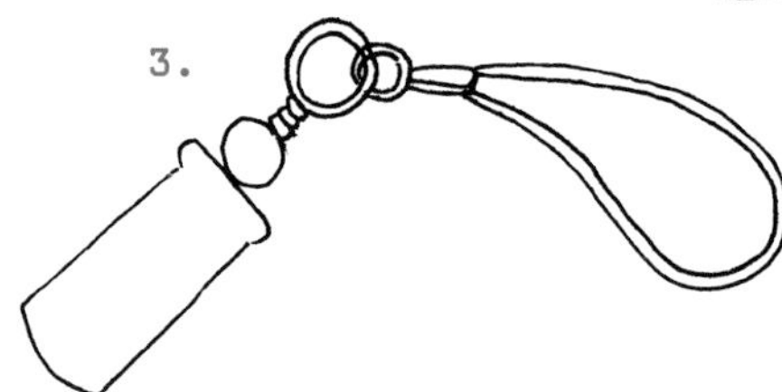

COMPONENTS AND HARDWARE

- 1 BLUE CAPACITOR {Radio Shack part number: 272-802}
- 1 4MM CLEAR SWAROVSKI BEAD
- 1 JUMP RING
- NEEDLE-NOSE PLIERS
- ROUND-NOSE PLIERS
- WIRE CUTTERS

Bar Code Charm

application

1. Slide three beads onto one lead of the orange-brown capacitor and two beads onto the second lead. Then try to do a capacitor wrap with the remaining portion of the leads as best you can (see page 26). (I know it's a little tricky!)

2. Finish by attaching the charm to the jump ring.

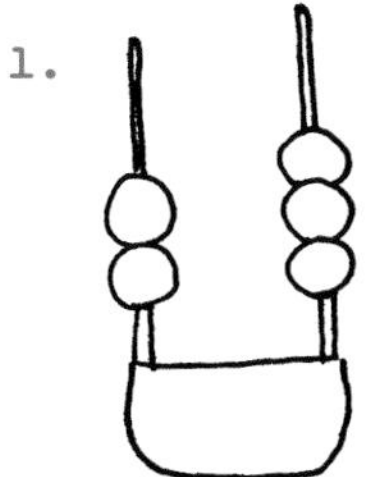

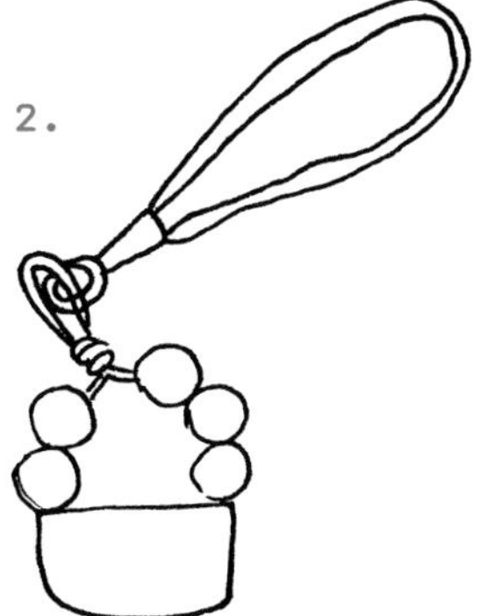

COMPONENTS AND HARDWARE

- > 1 MEDIUM ORANGE-BROWN CAPACITOR {Allied part number: 613-0546}
- > 2 4MM CLEAR SWAROVSKI BEADS
- > 3 4MM BLACK SWAROVSKI BEADS
- > 1 JUMP RING
- > NEEDLE-NOSE PLIERS
- > ROUND-NOSE PLIERS
- > WIRE CUTTERS

customizing your apps

- > **Paint the capacitors a solid color before assembling them.**
- > **Use seed beads instead of Swarovski crystals for a more everyday look.**
- > **Make a pair of charms and slide them onto a pair of hoop earrings.**

{medium}

Forget-Me-Not ID Holder

In these days of heightened security, chances are you have to wear an ID badge to school or work—so why not make it a statement? If you don't have an ID badge, use this holder to clip a few pens or even your reading glasses. There's always something you can hang around your neck!

COMPONENTS AND HARDWARE

- 35–40 SMALL TAN RESISTORS {Radio Shack part number: 271-308}
- 2 SMALL BLUE RESISTORS {Radio Shack part number: 272-309}
- 1 MEDIUM ORANGE-BROWN CAPACITOR {Allied part number: 613-0546}
- 8 4MM SWAROVSKI BEADS IN ASSORTED COLORS
- 8 INCHES {20.3 CM} 16-GAUGE JEWELRY WIRE
- /optional> 1 BADGE CLIP
- NEEDLE-NOSE PLIERS
- ROUND-NOSE PLIERS
- WIRE CUTTERS

more

PEAKS
PEAKS
ADULT 1064319138
RESORT CHARGE
Sarah
Gray

application

1. Take all the resistors and trim the leads to varying lengths, from ½ to 1 inch (1.3 to 2.5 cm). Select seven resistors and set them aside. Loop all the ends on the remaining resistors with your round-nose pliers.

2. Get the seven unlooped resistors and slide a Swarovski bead onto each of the leads, then loop the ends.

3. Chain all of the resistors together (see page 25), placing the resistors with beads randomly throughout. There is no clasp on this chain, so just chain the last two resistors together to close.

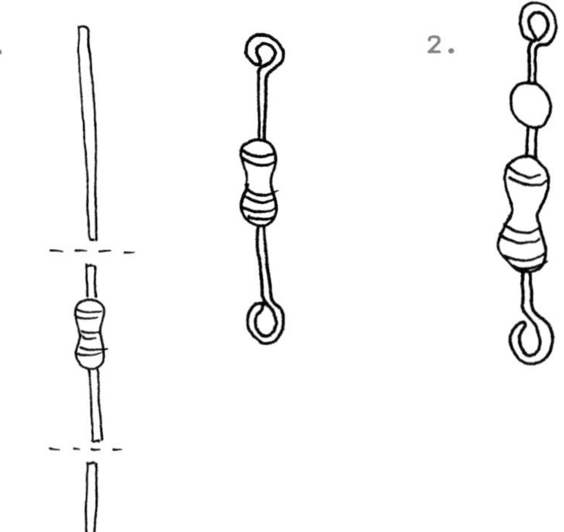

I was practically the only girl on campus who never lost her ID card—not while I had it attached to my Forget-Me-Not ID Holder!

4. Take your 16-gauge wire and something small and round, like a film canister or anything about 1½ inches (3.8 cm) in diameter. Leaving a 3-inch (7.6-cm) tail, wrap the wire around the small object two or three times.

5. Use the remaining wire to do a capacitor wrap (see page 26), then trim off the excess. Make a loop perpendicular to the main circle with your round-nose pliers.

6. Find the center of your chain and attach the wire circle you just made at the loop.

7. Take the orange-brown capacitor and do a capacitor wrap. Attach the loop to the wire circle.

8. Finish by snapping the badge holder onto your wire circle.

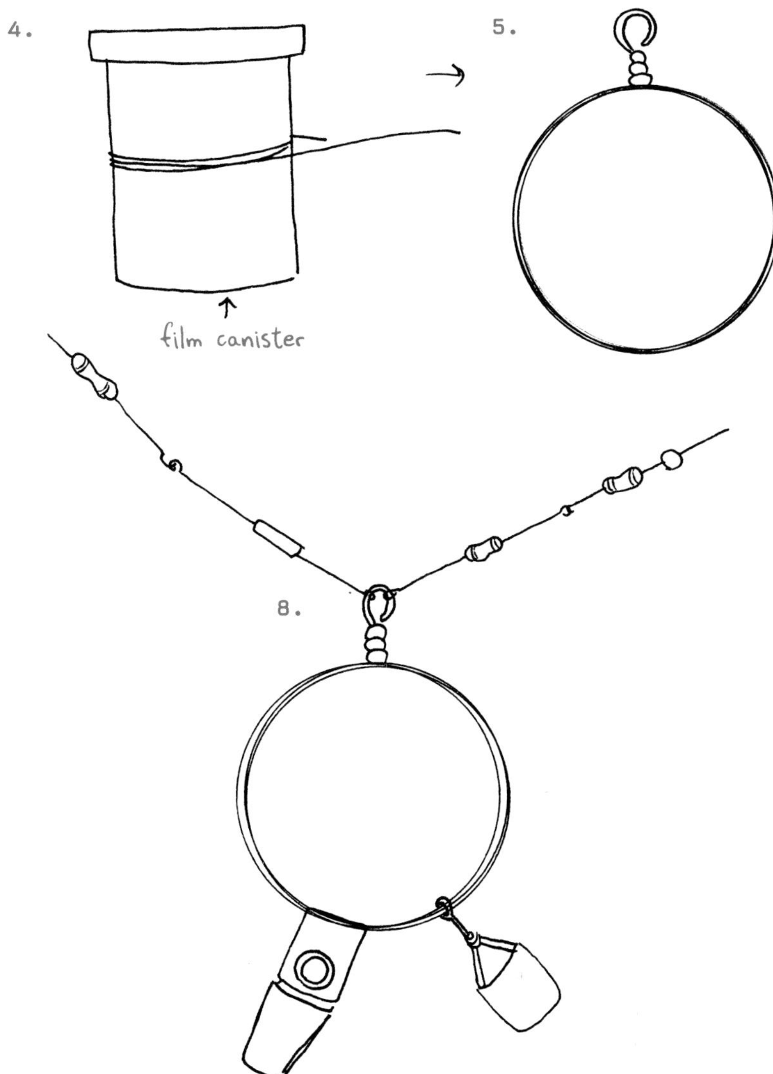

customizing your app

- Use capacitors in one color and omit the beads for a more masculine look.
- Add more charms to the wire circle at the bottom.
- Slide a bead onto each resistor.
- Use larger resistors for a more durable ID badge holder.

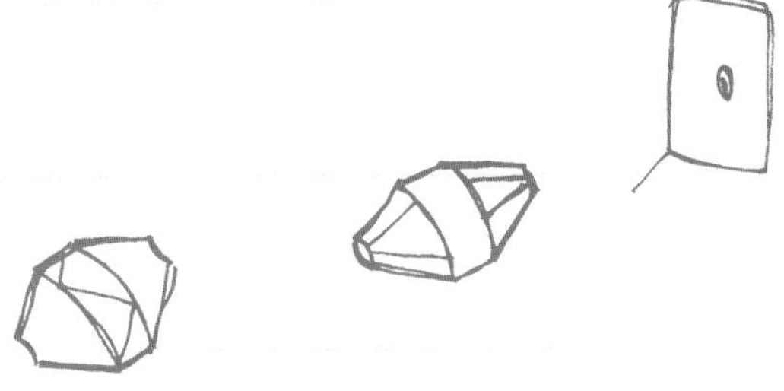

{hard}

Geeky Glasses Lanyard

"What happened to those glasses?" is something I think to myself almost every day. I lose my glasses a lot, and there just aren't many solutions for us younger folk. I made these holders for my sunglasses so I can take them off in class but keep them from getting scratched up in my bag. They're also a great gift for a mom or aunt who wears glasses and seems to have everything!

COMPONENTS AND HARDWARE

- 35–45 SMALL TAN RESISTORS {Radio Shack part number: 271-308}
- 4 SMALL BLUE RESISTORS {Radio Shack part number: 271-309}
- /optional> 1 TINY YELLOW CAPACITOR {Allied part number: 881-0417}
- /optional> 1 THERMISTOR DISC {Allied part number: 254-0036}
- /optional> 1 SMALL ORANGE CAPACITOR {Radio Shack part number: 272-131}
- /optional> 3 4MM SWAROVSKI BEADS IN ASSORTED COLORS
- 2 EYEGLASS HOLDERS {I got mine at Wal-Mart, but any craft store should have them}
- NEEDLE-NOSE PLIERS
- ROUND-NOSE PLIERS
- WIRE CLIPPERS

more

24"
18"

application

1. Take the small resistors and trim the leads uniformly to about ½ inch (1.3 cm) long. Loop all of the ends.

1.

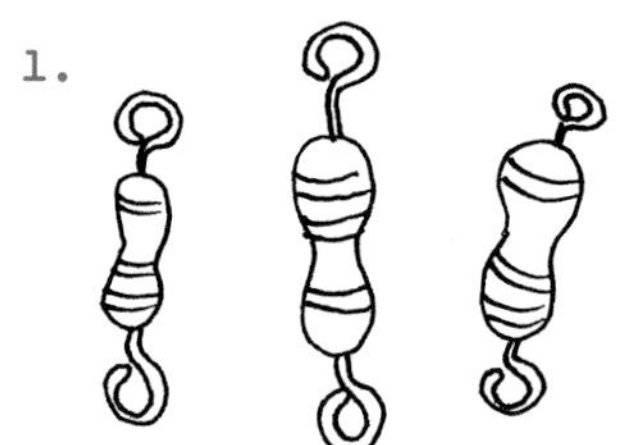

2. Chain all the resistors together (see page 25). When you're done, add an eyeglass holder at each end. You might want to test the length as you go to make sure it isn't too short or long. I suggest a length of at least 24 inches (61 cm).

2.

3. I just attached all sorts of excess components for this last step, so let your creativity go wild! Do the capacitor wrap on any capacitors to attach them (see page 26). To attach resistors, cut one lead completely off and loop the other end. You may also slide beads onto the leads before looping them. If you have long hair, I recommend adding charms only toward the ends; otherwise they'll get caught in your hair.

3.

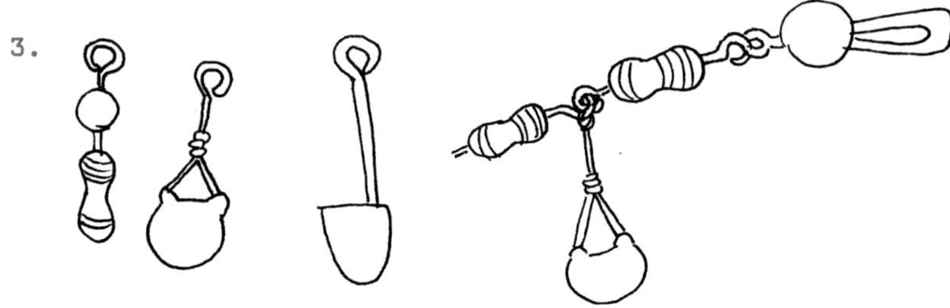

customizing your app

- **Slide beads onto your resistor chain.**
- **Add a large capacitor as a charm on one end.**

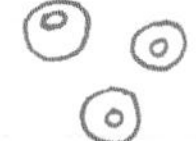

TOP 10 LIST NERDY BOOK SERIES

1. *The Dune Chronicles* by Frank Herbert
2. *Star Wars* by various authors
3. *The Lord of the Rings* by J.R.R. Tolkien
4. *The Chronicles of Narnia* by C.S. Lewis
5. *Ender's Game* by Orson Scott Card
6. *The Hitchhiker's Guide to the Galaxy* by Douglas Adams
7. *Foundation* by Issac Asimov
8. *Harry Potter* by J.K. Rowling
9. O'Reilly Media series by various authors
10. *The Dark Tower* by Stephen King

geeky glasses lanyard

The Geeky Glasses Lanyard not only helps me keep track of my glasses—it embodies everything I love about being geek chic! It's the perfect accessory for readers—whether your thang is science fiction or the Sunday comics.

Resources

The following are a few specific retailers that carry the electronic components and hardware that make up the jewelry in this book. Your best source for beads, tools, and jewelry findings is your local craft and/or beading store or any number of online jewelry crafting vendors.

> ALLIED ELECTRONICS
www.alliedelec.com

> FRY'S ELECTRONICS
www.frys.com

> RADIO SHACK
www.RadioShack.com

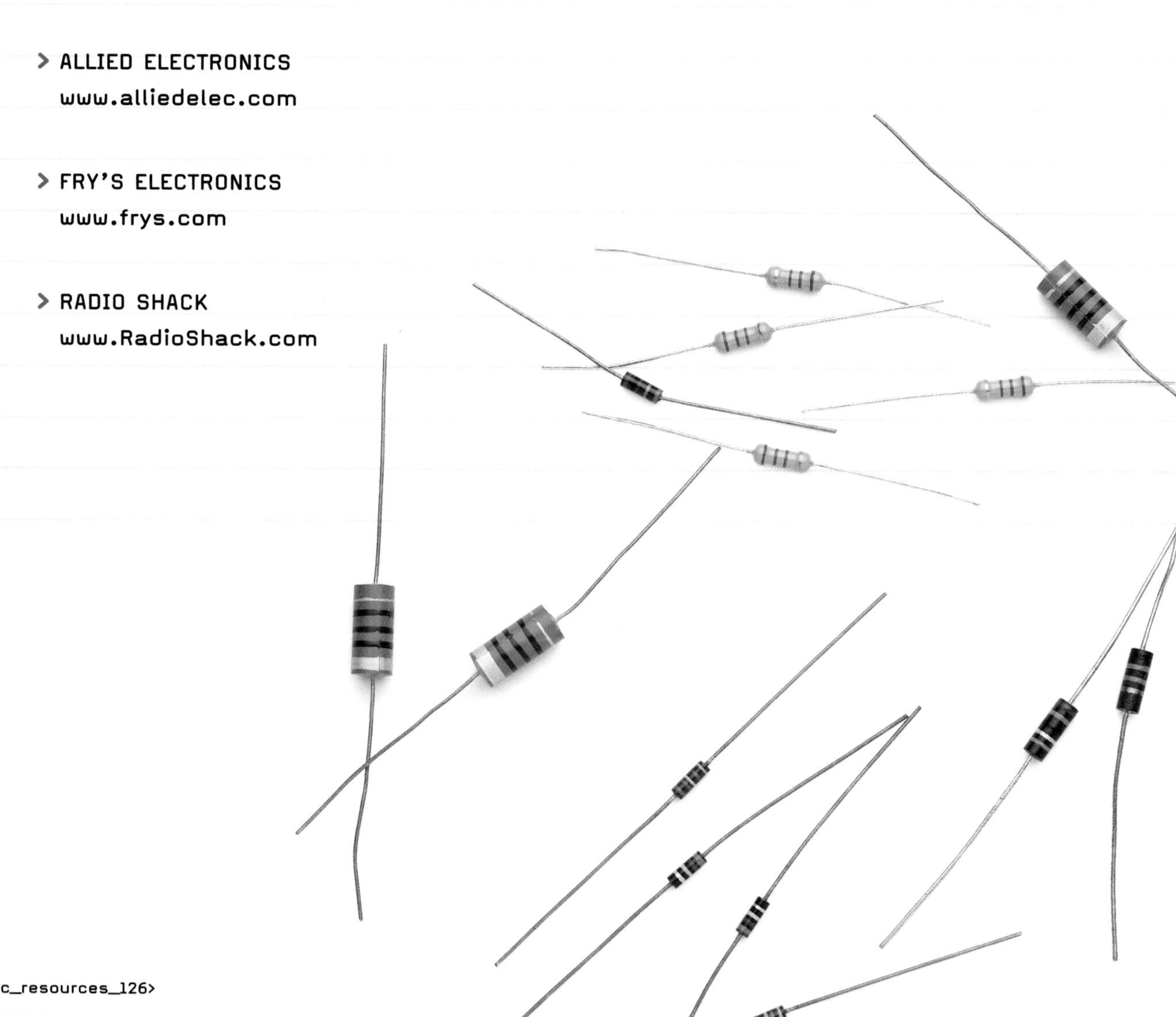

Index

more